On a Chinese Sc

On a Chinese Screen

W. Somerset Maugham

With an Introduction by H. J. Lethbridge

OXFORD
OXFORD UNIVERSITY PRESS
1985

Oxford University Press

Oxford London New York Toronto
Kuala Lumpur Singapore Hong Kong Tokyo
Delhi Bombay Calcutta Madras Karachi
Nairobi Dar es Salaam Cape Town
Melbourne Auckland

and associated companies in
Beirut Berlin Ibadan Mexico City Nicosia

First published by William Heinemann Limited in 1922
First issued, with permission and with the addition of an
Introduction, as an Oxford University Press paperback in 1985

ISBN 0 19 583863 7

Printed in Hong Kong

INTRODUCTION

Between the wars, Frenchmen believed that the greatest living English novelists were Charles Morgan and
Somerset Maugham. Today no one bothers with the
first — Morgan's literary reputation has plummeted
catastrophically — and it is doubtful if modern
Englishmen would place Maugham in English literature's first eleven, despite the fact that his works, and
his short stories in particular, are still popular.
Edmund Wilson, the great American critic, wrote: 'It
has happened to me from time to time to run into some
person of taste who tells me I ought to take Somerset
Maugham seriously, yet I have never been able to convince myself that he was anything but second-rate.'
Cyril Connolly took a different view and roundly
declared: 'Maugham is the greatest living short-story
writer.' Although his plays and novels (with the excep-
tion of *Cakes and Ale*) are no longer greatly esteemed,
his short stories, especially those set in the East, are
still much admired and he is often compared to Kipling
and to Maupassant, whose work inspired the young
Maugham. It is, one concludes, Maugham's connection
with the East, with South-east Asia, the Pacific
Islands, and China, that mostly attracts modern
readers.

William Somerset Maugham — 'Willie' to his friends
— was born in Paris in 1874, the son of a solicitor to the
British Embassy there. After his father's death (his
tubercular mother had died earlier), he was sent to live
with an uncle in England. At the age of 13 he entered

King's School, Canterbury. He did not go to university but, in 1892, began to attend lectures at St. Thomas's Hospital, London. His first novel, *Liza of Lambeth*, is based on his experiences as a hospital intern. He decided not to practise medicine after graduation but went to Seville to write, and his stay in Spain provided the material for his first travel book, *The Land of the Blessed Virgin*. Maugham was never poor but his success as a popular West End playwright soon made him very rich. In 1908 he had four plays running simultaneously in London, and thus broke all theatrical records.

With the outbreak of war in 1914, Maugham went to France as an ambulance driver. There Maugham first met Gerald Haxton, who was to become a lifelong friend. At that time Maugham was deeply in love with Syrie, the daughter of Dr Barnardo, the philanthropist. She was already married. While he waited for Syrie's divorce to come through, Maugham went off with Haxton to the United States and to the Pacific. In 1916 he returned to England and married. Soon after he was recruited by the British Secret Service as an agent and sent to Geneva, and in 1917 to Russia. He contracted tuberculosis there and returned with his lungs badly affected but recovered after a stay in a Scottish sanatorium. In September 1919 he set off, with Gerald Haxton, on his first visit to China. The following year, in October, he journeyed to Malaya, Indo-China, and again to China. Travel provided Maugham with plots and themes for his short stories, novels, and for two plays, *East of Suez* and *The Letter* (the latter a dramatization of a story first published in 1924).

Maugham, who suffered acutely from a stammer, was shy, withdrawn, sardonic, but highly observant. He found it difficult to enter into conversation with strangers, but Haxton was the opposite — a charming, good-looking extrovert American. In *The Summing-Up*, Maugham writes: 'I was fortunate enough to have on my journeys a companion who had an inestimable social gift ... through him I was able to get into easy contact with an immense number of persons whom otherwise I should have known only from a distance.' As Paul Fussell comments, 'Without a companion like Haxton, Maugham probably wouldn't have travelled at all.'

Gerald Haxton (1892–1944), who became Maugham's secretary and companion for nearly twenty-five years, was a homosexual. In 1915 Haxton was arrested in London on a charge of gross indecency, acquitted, but declared an undesirable alien. He could not return to England. This fact, so Maugham's biographers tell us, led Maugham to settle in France, and to acquire a villa at Cap Ferrat. Syrie Maugham, who made a great reputation in the Twenties as an interior decorator — she introduced all-white décor into the homes of the ultrasmart and the rich — divorced her husband in 1927. During the Second World War the two met at a party whereupon Syrie told him she was about to cross the Atlantic. She complained that she could not swim and would not know what to do if her ship were torpedoed. 'Ser-swallow', Willie stammered, 'Just ser-swallow'. Maugham did not like women very much.

Maugham was an intrepid traveller in the East. He used any form of available locomotion: donkey and bullock cart, canoe, sampan, and river-boat, tramp steamer and ocean liner. He stayed wherever it was possible to be put up, in clubhouse, planter's bungalow, mission station, official residence, or Chinese inn. He picked up the skeleton of many a story just listening to the conversations and gossip of those among whom he found himself. He was a good listener.

This is how he discovered the plot for his celebrated short story, *The Letter*, which was not only success- fully dramatized by Maugham himself but was also made into a film in 1940, with Bette Davis in the star- ring role. In 1911, a Mrs Ethel Proudlock had been accused of shooting her lover, William Steward, a mining engineer, in her Kuala Lumpur home. Her defence was that a drunken Steward had arrived unexpectedly and had attempted to rape her. She had shot him six times in order to defend her honour. This account was not believed and Mrs Proudlock was sentenced to death but later pardoned at the request of the Sultan of Selangor. In 1921, while visiting Kuala Lumpur, Maugham was the guest of one of Mrs Proud- lock's counsels in the trial and thus got hold of the facts behind the facts, which he filed away for literary purposes. The stories that Maugham wrote about South-east Asia and its expatriate communities angered many residents, particularly those who had given him much hospitality. In their eyes he was an ungentlemanly eavesdropper.

Some victims of Maugham's 'realism' responded with writs. One such was Arthur (later Sir Arthur) Fletcher, in 1925 the Acting Colonial Secretary of Hong Kong. When Fletcher read *The Painted Veil* he was outraged. In the opening chapter of the novel, the reader finds Kitty Fane, the heroine, in bed with Charles Townsend, Hong Kong's married Assistant Colonial Secretary, an unpleasant self-serving, self- regarding colonial official. As Maugham relates: 'It seemed to me strange that the temporary occupant of so insignificant a post should think himself aimed at, but in order to save trouble I changed Hong Kong to an imaginary colony of Tching-Yen.' Maugham originally had called his hero and heroine Lane but it appeared there were also people of that name in Hong

Kong. They brought an action, which was eventually settled for two hundred and fifty pounds. The book had already been published when Arthur Fletcher and the Lanes intervened. All copies of the novel were then called in but a few astute reviewers held on to theirs. These are now valuable properties, treasured by bibliophiles and collectors.

Maugham, to repeat, travelled to China in 1921 and this second visit inspired the composition of *On a Chinese Screen*. Prior to book publication, parts of the text appeared in *The American Bookman* and other periodicals. The book itself was first issued by George H. Doran, Maugham's American publisher, in October 1922; a month later the first English edition appeared under the imprint of William Heinemann, his English publisher. In 1925 Heinemann included it as a volume in his popular Traveller's Library series. It was well reviewed.

Dedicated to Syrie, *On a Chinese Screen* is a potpourri of sketches and vignettes, and also includes two short stories, *The Taipan* and *The Consul*. The former is a ghost story, the atmosphere of which is reminiscent of Sheridan Le Fanu; the latter is a gentler, even comic, story of an English girl married to a returned Chinese student. She lives in a polygamous Chinese household and experiences all the rigours of traditional Chinese domestic life. Included in the book are also a number of very short pieces which read like prose poems or invocations to nature or to Pan. Maugham was influenced, one knows, by what he believed was the tone and texture of classical Chinese writing, but he could not read Chinese.

In China Maugham met specimens of the taipan class, merchants, Legation and Consular officials, and scholars, all those who formed the upper levels or apex of the expatriate community and who foregathered as equals in the club, for that institution, as George Orwell writes in *Burmese Days*, was the true centre of European life in the East. Its membership was always carefully prescribed; the ill-bred and the bounder brigade were usually blackballed. Lower down in the pecking order were missionaries (always difficult to position in any Eastern country), journalists (some very rum fellows indeed), commercial agents of all types, various subordinate employees of commercial firms, teachers, and possibly nurses. The lower middle class was represented, as it were, by ships' captains, ships' engineers, tide-waiters in the Chinese Maritime Customs Service, and in Shanghai and Hong Kong by those employed in the public utilities. The bottom strata contained the great European unwashed — the unemployed and unemployable — beachcombers, spongers, derelicts, and alcoholics, but also prostitutes, who were normally well-washed and much-scented. Apart from the intrinsic merit and charm of some of the sketches, *On a Chinese Screen* is valuable for the historian and sociologist. It is full of sharp observations on the life, manners, and attitudes of the expatriate community. Maugham had no axe to grind in China. He did not bring tidings of reform or regeneration. He had no theme to expound to dumbfounded Chinese: he came simply to look at life and to record and relate his impressions.

On the whole, it appears he did not care much for the Europeans he met. Of the business community he wrote: 'They talked of racing and golf and shooting. They would have thought it bad form to touch upon the abstract and there was no politics for them to discuss. China bored them all, they did not want to speak of that; they only knew just so much about it as was necessary to their business, and they looked with distrust upon any man who studies the Chinese language. Why should he unless he were a missionary or a Chinese Secretary at the Legation?' In another sketch Maugham writes of a taipan: 'He had been in China for thirty years, and he prided himself on not speaking a word of Chinese. He never went into the Chinese city ... But if you wanted him to talk to you about London he was prepared to do so by the hour.'

He also had a low opinion of most missionaries. He describes them as ignorant, uneducated, incurious, self-satisfied, and patronizing to those among whom they lived. He was quick to detect their neuroses, their quirks and tics. But he did admire Catholic priests and nuns for their unselfishness and desire to serve the Chinese. Protestant missionaries in the main were not highly educated and most were lower middle class in origin; their social manners were very chapel, and the women too often plain, ungainly, and gauche. All were teetotal, and all spoke vehemently against the sins of the flesh. The Catholics, in Maugham's eyes, were far more civilized and tolerant, and probably better bred. Maugham was a snob, a scion of the Victorian professional classes.

It is not easy to chart precisely Maugham's itinerary from his text but it is likely he came by boat from Saigon or Haiphong, then under French administration, to Hong Kong; and by sea again to Shanghai, a good staging post for China travel. It is clear that he stayed in Peking and visited Tientsin. One infers that after exploring parts of northern China and the verges of Mongolia he returned to Shanghai, at the mouth of the Yangtse, and went up that great river by steamer to Chungking.

Outside a few large towns such as Peking, the treaty port of Shanghai and the colony of Hong Kong, Europeans were sparse. Most lived remote and isolated lives. It must have been awful for them to see the same few European faces day after day, at work or at play. Boredom was an acute problem, especially for wives, and recourse to the bottle could not always provide medicine for melancholy. The married had to undergo the additional ordeal of sending their children back to England for education, and for their health, at the age of 7 or 8. (The less well-to-do might send their children to schools in Shanghai or Hong Kong, or to Weihaiwei where a European school had been opened.) Home leave was usually every five years, but a wife normally stayed on longer in England than her husband. Travel was restricted in the First World War and Maugham describes the state of mind of one expatriate who had not seen his daughter for over eight years: now she was grown up, and married to a strange man. The general impression the reader is likely to get of European life is one of great sadness, hardly compensated for by high salaries, of great emotional waste and spiritual attrition, certainly in the out-ports and smaller European communities. And it was not uncommon to die suddenly and mysteriously, like the Taipan in Maugham's story, in a foreign land, long before retirement to the Home Counties.

Maugham could not speak Chinese; the vast majority of Chinese could not speak English. So he met far fewer Chinese than Europeans. But he does tell of nice encounters with a cabinet minister, a philosopher, and a Professor of Comparative Modern Literature, all Chinese. These are among the best vignettes in the book, meetings in which the native usually scores off the foreigner. Ever present in *On a Chinese Screen* are China's myriad toilers, the coolie and the rickshaw-puller — beasts of burden — and these Maugham clearly admired and commiserated with. There are also several sketches of Continentals, of members of the *corps diplomatique*, of the tweedledees and tweedledums of the various European legations, men obsessed with notions of decorum, conduct, and protocol. The account of the astute M. de Steenvoorde, more wittol than cuckold, who claims a sum of money from his parents-in-law each time his wife takes a new lover, is extremely funny: 'M. de Steenvoorde is already a man of means, but before his wife reaches the canonical age he will undoubtedly be a rich one.'

The short bibliography appended to this introduction includes all of Maugham's works that relate to the East. In 1930 he produced another travel book, *The Gentleman in the Parlour*, subtitled *A Record of a Journey from Rangoon to Haiphong*. *The Razor's Edge* (1944), his bestselling novel, had an Indian rather than Chinese locale, for its theme is mysticism or mystical states. *A Writer's Notebook*, a compilation of extracts from his many diaries, contains much material on the Pacific (Oceania), South-east Asia, and China. After the end of the Second World War he did not return to China: conditions in that country were chaotic and there was conflict between Nationalists and Communists. But the real reason Maugham travelled less widely after 1945 was not simply age — he was 61 in 1945 — but because Gerald Haxton had died in New York in 1944, his end hastened by alcoholism. *A Writer's Notebook* carries the dedication: 'In Loving Memory of My Friend Gerald Frederick Haxton, 1892-1944'. If Maugham had ever deeply loved any human being it was certainly Haxton, whom he had helped to extricate from many a scrape. One night, at Cap Ferrat, a drunken Haxton had dived fully-clothed into Maugham's empty swimming-pool. With medical help and Maugham's care, the inert secretary was resurrected. Once Maugham lost this charming and gay companion, his desire to go to faraway places weakened, as Fussell hints.

There is a well-known portrait of Maugham by Graham Sutherland, now in the Tate Gallery in London. Sutherland has given the distinguished author a shrunken lizard-like face. The eyes are sardonic and hooded, the half-smile sarcastic. But, as many have noticed, the general impression is that of an Oriental saint, a Taoist sage, contemplating the flow of time and meditating on the meaning of life. In *Of Human Bondage*, Maugham's long autobiographical novel, the hero, Philip, is given a Persian carpet and told that it contains the secret of life. Only much later does Philip come to realize that the pattern is only a pattern, that it is meaningless.

When Syrie died in 1954, Maugham wrote to a close friend: 'It would be hypocrisy on my part to pretend that I am deeply grieved at Syrie's death.' After their divorce in 1927, they met on only a few occasions, usually by chance. Oddly, his hatred for her increased over the years, possibly, as his biographers suggest, because he came to believe she had gossiped too much in Mayfair drawing-rooms about his long homosexual liaison with Gerald Haxton: in 1927 he had dissuaded her from citing his companion as co-respondent. Maugham, in modern idiom, never came out of the closet. He was a late Victorian and had been deeply disquieted by the Oscar Wilde scandal. He always wished to maintain in public a completely respectable façade.

Towards the end of his life, Maugham's mind became clouded and obsessed. He imagined he was not the legal father of his daughter Liza (named after the eponymous heroine of his first novel) and he took steps to disinherit her. Eventually he saw reason, and matters were arranged between them. Maugham died in 1965, two months short of his ninety-second birthday, in the Anglo-American Hospital in Nice. His ashes were buried in the grounds of King's School, Canterbury, his old school, where he had spent many unhappy days because of his stammer and frail physique.

Maugham's literary reputation remains uncertain, controversial. A few of his short stories such as *The Letter*, *Rain*, *The Outstation*, *The Vessel of Wrath*, and some others, have achieved 'classic' status and are much anthologized. He greatly admired Kipling but never wrote a story as moving or as satisfying as Kipling's *On Greenhow Hill*, *Without Benefit of Clergy*, or *The Man Who Would Be King*; nor one as complex as Conrad's *The Secret Sharer* or *The Heart of Darkness*. Maugham lacked Kipling's insight into native races and Conrad's penetration of the Eastern psyche. Maugham's fundamental weakness is that he did not care deeply about his characters; and this reflected not only his ingrained misogyny but also his dislike of people. At the Villa Mauresque, he would greet visitors with welcoming arms, and then drop them as they came close: he shied away from human contact. Today we like our writers to be committed, involved, and to exhibit sympathy. But Maugham seems rather too detached. Early in life his emotions atrophied, when his mother died: he never recovered from that childhood betrayal.

On a Chinese Screen, closer to reportage or documentary than fiction, is still highly readable. It has pathos and comedy. It describes with great skill how Europeans once lived in China. This book, one surmises, will survive far longer than most of his novels and his once fashionable plays.

H.J. LETHBRIDGE

BIBLIOGRAPHY

Allen, Charles (ed.), *Tales From the South China Seas* (London, André Deutsch, 1983).

Allen, G.C., and Donnithorne, Audrey G., *Western Enterprise in Far Eastern Economic Development* (London, George Allen & Unwin, 1964).

Arlington, L.C., *Through the Dragon's Eyes: Fifty Years' Experience of a Foreigner in the Chinese Government Service* (London, Constable, 1931).

Butcher, John G., *The British in Malaya, 1880–1941* (Kuala Lumpur, Oxford University Press, 1979).

Collis, Maurice, *Trials in Burma* (London, Faber and Faber, 1938).

Connolly, Cyril, 'The Art of Being Good', in *The Condemned Playground. Essays: 1927–1944* (New York, The Macmillan Company, 1946), pp. 250–9.

Cordell, Richard A., *Somerset Maugham: A Writer for all Seasons* (Bloomington, Indiana, Indiana University Press, 1969).

Fauconnier, Henri, *Malaisie* (Paris, Arthème Fayard, 1930), translated as *The Soul of Malaya* (London, E. Mathews & Marrot, 1931).

Fussell, Paul, *Abroad: British Literary Travelling Between the Wars* (New York, Oxford University Press, 1980).

Hergé, *Le Lotus Bleu* (Paris, Casterman, 1946).

King, Paul, *In the Chinese Customs Service: A Personal Record of Forty-Seven Years* (London, T. Fisher Unwin, 1924).

Maugham, Robin, *Somerset and All the Maughams* (London, Heinemann, 1966).

Morgan, Ted, *Somerset Maugham* (London, Jonathan Cape, 1980).

Nichols, Beverley, *A Case of Human Bondage* (London, Secker & Warburg, 1966).

Orwell, George, *Burmese Days* (London, Victor Gollancz, 1935).

Purcell, Victor, *The Memoirs of a Malayan Official* (London, Cassell, 1965).

Sherry, Norman, 'How murder on the veranda inspired Somerset Maugham', *Observer Magazine*, 22 February 1976.

Woodcock, George, *The British in the Far East* (London, Weidenfeld and Nicolson, 1969).

Wilson, Edmund, *Classics and Commercials* (London, W.H. Allen, 1951).

The following select bibliography includes all Maugham's works on the East and others referred to in the Introduction.

Maugham, William Somerset, *Liza of Lambeth* (London, T. Fisher Unwin, 1897).

_____ *The Land of the Blessed Virgin: Sketches and Impressions in Andalusia* (London, William Heinemann, 1905).

_____ *The Moon and Sixpence* (London, William Heinemann, 1919).

_____ *The Trembling of a Leaf* (London, William Heinemann, 1921).

_____ *East of Suez: A Play in Seven Scenes* (London, William Heinemann, 1922).

_____ *The Painted Veil* (London, William Heinemann, 1925).

——— *The Casuarina Tree: Six Stories* (London, William Heinemann, 1926).

——— *The Letter: A Play in Three Acts* (London, William Heinemann, 1927).

——— *Cakes and Ale* (London, William Heinemann, 1930).

——— *The Gentleman in the Parlour: A Record of a Journey from Rangoon to Haiphong* (London, William Heinemann, 1930).

——— *The Narrow Corner* (London, William Heinemann, 1932).

——— *Ah King* (London, William Heinemann, 1933).

——— *The Summing Up* (London, William Heinemann, 1938).

——— *The Razor's Edge* (London, William Heinemann, 1944).

——— *A Writer's Notebook* (London, William Heinemann, 1949).

ON A CHINESE SCREEN

BY

W. SOMERSET MAUGHAM

LONDON: WILLIAM HEINEMANN

FOR
SYRIE

CONTENTS

		PAGE
I	THE RISING OF THE CURTAIN	11
II	MY LADY'S PARLOUR	14
III	THE MONGOL CHIEF	17
IV	THE ROLLING STONE	19
V	THE CABINET MINISTER	23
VI	DINNER PARTIES	27
VII	THE ALTAR OF HEAVEN	33
VIII	THE SERVANTS OF GOD	35
IX	THE INN	40
X	THE GLORY HOLE	44
XI	FEAR	47
XII	THE PICTURE	55
XIII	HER BRITANNIC MAJESTY'S REPRESENTATIVE	57
XIV	THE OPIUM DEN	60
XV	THE LAST CHANCE	62
XVI	THE NUN	64
XVII	HENDERSON	66
XVIII	DAWN	70
XIX	THE POINT OF HONOUR	73
XX	THE BEAST OF BURDEN	77
XXI	DR. MACALISTER	80
XXII	THE ROAD	85
XXIII	GOD'S TRUTH	90
XXIV	ROMANCE	94
XXV	THE GRAND STYLE	99
XXVI	RAIN	103
XXVII	SULLIVAN	107

CONTENTS

		PAGE
XXVIII	THE DINING-ROOM	109
XXIX	ARABESQUE	113
XXX	THE CONSUL	114
XXXI	THE STRIPLING	122
XXXII	THE FANNINGS	124
XXXIII	THE SONG OF THE RIVER	129
XXXIV	MIRAGE	131
XXXV	THE STRANGER	134
XXXVI	DEMOCRACY	140
XXXVII	THE SEVENTH DAY ADVENTIST	144
XXXVIII	THE PHILOSOPHER	147
XXXIX	THE MISSIONARY LADY	159
XL	A GAME OF BILLIARDS	162
XLI	THE SKIPPER	164
XLII	THE SIGHTS OF THE TOWN	166
XLIII	NIGHTFALL	171
XLIV	THE NORMAL MAN	173
XLV	THE OLD TIMER	179
XLVI	THE PLAIN	183
XLVII	FAILURE	186
XLVIII	A STUDENT OF THE DRAMA	188
XLIX	THE TAIPAN	193
L	METEMPSYCHOSIS	204
LI	THE FRAGMENT	206
LII	ONE OF THE BEST	211
LIII	THE SEA-DOG	214
LIV	THE QUESTION	221
LV	THE SINOLOGUE	223
LVI	THE VICE-CONSUL	225
LVII	A CITY BUILT ON A ROCK	231
LVIII	A LIBATION TO THE GODS	236

ON A CHINESE SCREEN

ON A CHINESE SCREEN

I

THE RISING OF THE CURTAIN

YOU come to the row of hovels that leads to the gate of the city. They are built of dried mud and so dilapidated that you feel a breath of wind will lay them flat upon the dusty earth from which they have been made. A string of camels, heavily laden, steps warily past you. They wear the disdainful air of profiteers forced to traverse a world in which many people are not so rich as they. A little crowd, tattered in their blue clothes, is gathered about the gate and it scatters as a youth in a pointed cap gallops up on a Mongolian pony. A band of children are chasing a lame dog and they throw clods of mud at it. Two stout gentlemen in long black gowns of figured silk and silk jackets stand talking to one another. Each holds a little stick, perched on which, with a string attached to its leg, is a little bird. They have brought out their pets for an airing and in friendly fashion compare their merits. Now and then the birds give a flutter into the air, the length of the string, and return quickly to their perch. The two Chinese gentlemen, smiling, look at them with soft eyes. Rude boys cry out at the foreigner in a shrill and scornful voice. The city wall, crumbling, old and crenellated, looks like the city wall in an old picture of some Palestinish town of the Crusaders.

You pass through the gateway into a narrow street lined with shops: many of them with their elegant lattice work, red and gold, and their elaborate carving, have a peculiar ruined magnificence, and you imagine that in their dark recesses are sold all manner of strange wares of the fabulous East. A great multitude surges along the uneven narrow footwalk or in the deepset street; and coolies, bearing heavy loads, shout for way in short sharp cries. Hawkers with guttural sound call their wares.

And now at a sedate pace, drawn by a sleek mule, comes a Peking cart. Its hood is bright blue and its great wheels are studded with nails. The driver sits with dangling legs on a shaft. It is evening and the sun sets red behind the yellow, steep, and fantastic roof of a temple. The Peking cart, the blind in front drawn down, passes silently and you wonder who it is that sits cross-legged within. Perhaps it is a scholar, all the learning of the classics at his finger ends, bound on a visit to a friend with whom he will exchange elaborate compliments and discuss the golden age of Tang and Sung which can return no more; perhaps it is a singing girl in splendid silks and richly

12

embroidered coat, with jade in her black hair, summoned to a party so that she may sing a little song and exchange elegant repartee with young blades cultured enough to appreciate wit. The Peking cart disappears into the gathering darkness: it seems to carry all the mystery of the East.

II

MY LADY'S PARLOUR

I REALLY think I can make something of it," she said.

She looked about her briskly, and the light of the creative imagination filled her eyes with brightness.

It was an old temple, a small one, in the city, which she had taken and was turning into a dwelling house. It had been built for a very holy monk by his admirers three hundred years before, and here in great piety, practising innumerable austerities, he had passed his declining days. For long after in memory of his virtue the faithful had come to worship, but in course of time funds had fallen very low and at last the two or three monks that remained were forced to leave. It was weather-beaten and the green tiles of the roof were overgrown with weeds. The raftered ceiling was still beautiful with its faded gold dragons on a faded red; but she did not like a dark ceiling, so she stretched a canvas across and papered it. Needing air and sunlight, she cut two large windows on one side. She very luckily had some blue curtains which were just the right size. Blue was her favourite colour: it brought out the colour of

14

her eyes. Since the columns, great red sturdy columns, oppressed her a little she papered them with a very nice paper which did not look Chinese at all. She was lucky also with the paper with which she covered the walls. It was bought in a native shop, but really it might have come from Sandersons'; it was a very nice pink stripe and it made the place look cheerful at once. At the back was a recess in which had stood a great lacquer table and behind it an image of the Buddha in his eternal meditation. Here generations of believers had burned their tapers and prayed, some for this temporal benefit or that, some for release from the returning burden of earthly existence; and this seemed to her the very place for an American stove. She was obliged to buy her carpet in China, but she managed to get one that looked so like an Axminster that you would hardly know the difference. Of course, being hand-made, it had not quite the smoothness of the English article, but it was a very decent substitute. She was able to buy a very nice lot of furniture from a member of the Legation who was leaving the country for a post in Rome, and she got a nice bright chintz from Shanghai to make loose covers with. Fortunately she had quite a number of pictures, wedding presents and some even that she had bought herself, for she was very artistic, and these gave the room a cosy look. She needed a screen and here there was no help for it, she had to buy a Chinese one, but as she very cleverly said, you might perfectly well have a Chi-

15

nese screen in England. She had a great many photographs, in silver frames, one of them of a Princess of Schleswig-Holstein, and one of the Queen of Sweden, both signed, and these she put on the grand piano, for they give a room an air of being lived in. Then, having finished, she surveyed her work with satisfaction.

"Of course it doesn't look like a room in London," she said, "but it might quite well be a room in some nice place in England, Cheltenham, say, or Tunbridge Wells."

III

THE MONGOL CHIEF

HEAVEN knows from what mysterious distance he had come. He rode down the winding pathway from the high Mongolian plateau with the mountains, barren, stony, and inaccessible, stretching on all sides, an impenetrable barrier; he rode down past the temple that guarded the head of the pass till he came to the old river bed which was the gateway into China. It was hedged in by the foothills brilliant under the morning sun, with sharp shadows; and the innumerable traffic of the centuries had formed on that stony floor a rough road. The air was keen and clear, the sky was blue. Here all the year round from daybreak till sundown, passed an unending stream, camels in caravan bearing the brick tea to Urga seven hundred miles away and so to Siberia, long lines of wagons drawn by placid bullocks, and little carts in twos and threes behind stout ponies; and in the contrary direction, into China, again camels in caravan bringing hides to the markets of Peking, and wagons in long procession. Now a mob of horses went by and then a flock of goats. But his eyes did not rest on the various scene. He seemed not to notice that others were travelling the pass. He was accompanied by his henchmen, six or seven of them, somewhat bedraggled it is true, on sorry nags, but they had a truculent air. They ambled along in a slovenly bunch. He was dressed in a black silk coat and black silk trousers thrust into his long riding boots with their turned-up toes, and on his head he wore the high sable cap of his country. He held himself erect, riding a little ahead of his followers, proudly, and as he rode, his head high and his eyes steady, you wondered if he thought that down this pass in days gone by his ancestors had ridden, ridden down upon the fertile plain of China where rich cities lay ready to their looting.

IV

THE ROLLING STONE

I HEARD his extraordinary story before I
I saw him and I expected someone of strik-
ing appearance. It seemed to me that anyone who had gone through such singular
experiences must have in his outer man something
singular too. But I found a person in whose
aspect there was nothing remarkable. He was
smaller than the average, somewhat frail, sun-
burned, with hair beginning to turn grey though
he was still under thirty, and brown eyes. He
looked like anybody else, and you might see
him half a dozen times before remembering who
he was. If you had happened upon him behind
the counter of a department store or on a stool in
a broker's office you would have thought him perfectly in place. But you would have noticed him
as little as you noticed the counter or the stool.
There was so little in him to attract attention
that in the end it became intriguing: his face,
empty of significance, reminded you of the blank
wall of a Manchu palace, in a sordid street, behind which you knew were painted courtyards,
carved dragons, and heaven knows what subtle
intricacy of life.

For his whole career was remarkable. The son of a veterinary surgeon, he had been a reporter in the London police courts and then had gone as steward on board a merchant ship to Buenos Ayres. There he had deserted and somehow or other had worked his way across South America. From a port in Chili he managed to get to the Marquesas where for six months he had lived on the natives always ready to offer hospitality to a white man, and then, begging a passage on a schooner to Tahiti, had shipped to Amoy as second mate of an old tub which carried Chinese labour to the Society Islands.

That was nine years before I met him and since then he had lived in China. First he got work with the B. A. T. Company, but after a couple of years he found it monotonous; and having acquired a certain knowledge of the language he entered the employment of a firm which distributed patent medicines through the length and breadth of the land. For three years he wandered in province after province, selling pills, and at the end of it had saved eight hundred dollars. He cut himself adrift once more.

He began then the most remarkable of his adventures. He set out from Peking on a journey right across the country, travelling in the guise of a poor Chinaman, with his roll of bedding, his Chinese pipe, and his tooth-brush. He stayed in the Chinese inns, sleeping on the kangs huddled up with fellow wayfarers, and ate the Chinese food. This alone is no mean feat. He used the train but little, going for the most part on foot, by cart, or by river. He went through Shensi and Shansi; he walked on the windy plateaus of Mongolia and risked his life in barbaric Turkestan; he spent long weeks with the nomads of the desert and travelled with the caravans that carried the brick tea across the arid wilderness of Gobi. At last, four years later, having spent his last dollar he reached Peking once more.

He set about looking for a job. The easiest way to earn money seemed to write, and the editor of one of the English papers in China offered to take a series of articles on his journey. I suppose his only difficulty was to choose from the fulness of his experience. He knew much which he was perhaps the only Englishman to know. He had seen all manner of things, quaint, impressive, terrible, amusing, and unexpected. He wrote twenty-four articles. I will not say that they were unreadable, for they showed a careful and a sympathetic observation; but he had seen everything at haphazard, as it were, and they were but the material of art. They were like the catalogue of the Army and Navy Stores, a mine to the imaginative man, but the foundation of literature rather than literature itself. He was the field naturalist who patiently collects an infinity of facts, but has no gift for generalisation: they remain facts that await the synthesis of minds more complicated than his. He collected neither plants nor beasts, but men. His collection was unrivalled, but his knowledge of it slender.

When I met him I sought to discern how the variety of his experience had affected him; but though he was full of anecdote, a jovial, friendly creature, willing to talk at length of all he had seen, I could not discover that any of his adventures had intimately touched him. The instinct to do all the queer things he had done showed that there was in him a streak of queerness. The civilised world irked him and he had a passion to get away from the beaten trail. The oddities of life amused him. He had an insatiable curiosity. But I think his experiences were merely of the body and were never translated into experiences of the soul. Perhaps that is why at bottom you felt he was commonplace. The insignificance of his mien was a true index to the insignificance of his soul. Behind the blank wall was blankness.

That was certainly why with so much to write about he wrote tediously, for in writing the important thing is less richness of material than richness of personality.

V

THE CABINET MINISTER

HE received me in a long room looking on to a sandy garden. The roses withered on the stunted bushes and the great old trees flagged forlorn. He sat me down on a square stool at a square table and took his seat in front of me. A servant brought cups of flowered tea and American cigarettes. He was a thin man, of the middle height, with thin, elegant hands; and through his gold-rimmed spectacles he looked at me with large, dark, and melancholy eyes. He had the look of a student or of a dreamer. His smile was very sweet. He wore a brown silk gown and over it a short black silk jacket, and on his head a billy-cock hat.

"Is it not strange," he said, with his charming smile, "that we Chinese wear this gown because three hundred years ago the Manchus were horsemen?"

"Not so strange," I retorted, "as that because the English won the battle of Waterloo Your Excellency should wear a bowler."

"Do you think that is why I wear it?"

"I could easily prove it."

Since I was afraid that his exquisite courtesy would prevent him from asking me how, I hastened in a few well-chosen words to do so.

He took off his hat and looked at it with the shadow of a sigh. I glanced round the room. It had a green Brussels carpet, with great flowers on it, and round the walls were highly carved black-wood chairs. From a picture rail hung scrolls on which were writings by the great masters of the past, and to vary these, in bright gold frames, were oil paintings which in the nineties might very well have been exhibited in the Royal Academy. The minister did his work at an American roll-top desk.

He talked to me with melancholy of the state of China. A civilisation, the oldest the world had known, was now being ruthlessly swept away. The students who came back from Europe and from America were tearing down what endless generations had built up, and they were placing nothing in its stead. They had no love of their country, no religion, no reverence. The temples, deserted by worshipper and priest, were falling into decay and presently their beauty would be nothing but a memory.

But then, with a gesture of his thin, aristocratic hands, he put the subject aside. He asked me whether I would care to see some of his works of art. We walked round the room and he showed me priceless porcelains, bronzes, and Tang figures. There was a horse from a grave in Honan which had the grace and the exquisite modelling

of a Greek work. On a large table by the side
of his desk was a number of rolls. He chose one
and holding it at the top gave it to me to unroll.
It was a picture of some early dynasty of mountains seen through fleecy clouds, and with smiling
eyes he watched my pleasure as I looked. The
picture was set aside and he showed me another
and yet another. Presently I protested that I
could not allow a busy man to waste his time on
me, but he would not let me go. He brought out
picture after picture. He was a connoisseur. He
was pleased to tell me the schools and periods to
which they belonged and neat anecdotes about
their painters.

"I wish I could think it was possible for you
to appreciate my greatest treasures," he said,
pointing to the scrolls that adorned his walls.
"Here you have examples of the most perfect
calligraphies of China."

"Do you like them better than paintings?" I
asked.

"Infinitely. Their beauty is more chaste.
There is nothing meretricious in them. But I can
quite understand that a European would have
difficulty in appreciating so severe and so delicate
an art. Your taste in Chinese things tends a little
to the grotesque, I think."

He produced books of paintings and I turned
their leaves. Beautiful things! With the dramatic instinct of the collector he kept to the last
the book by which he set most store. It was a
series of little pictures of birds and flowers,

roughly done with a few strokes, but with such a power of suggestion, with so great a feeling for nature and such a playful tenderness, that it took your breath away. There were sprigs of plum-blossom that held in their dainty freshness all the magic of the spring; there were sparrows in whose ruffled plumage were the beat and the tremor of life. It was the work of a great artist.

"Will these American students ever produce anything like this?" he asked with a rueful smile.

But to me the most charming part of it was that I knew all the time that he was a rascal. Corrupt, inefficient, and unscrupulous, he let nothing stand in his way. He was a master of the squeeze. He had acquired a large fortune by the most abominable methods. He was dishonest, cruel, vindictive, and venal. He had certainly had a share in reducing China to the desperate plight which he so sincerely lamented. But when he held in his hand a little vase of the colour of lapis lazuli his fingers seemed to curl about it with a charming tenderness, his melancholy eyes caressed it as they looked, and his lips were slightly parted as though with a sigh of desire.

VI

DINNER PARTIES

I: LEGATION QUARTER

THE Swiss director of the Banque Sino-Argentine was announced. He came with a large, handsome wife, who displayed her opulent charms so generously that it made you a little nervous. It was said that she had been a *cocotte*, and an English maiden lady (in salmon pink satin and beads) who had come early, greeted her with a thin and frigid smile. The Minister of Guatemala and the Chargé d'Affaires of Montenegro entered together. The Chargé d'Affaires was in a state of extreme agitation; he had not understood that it was an official function, he thought he had been asked to dine *en petit comité*, and he had not put on his orders. And there was the Minister of Guatemala blazing with stars! What in heaven's name was to be done? The emotion caused by what for a moment seemed almost a diplomatic incident was diverted by the appearance of two Chinese servants in long silk robes and four-sided hats with cocktails and zakouski. Then a Russian princess sailed in. She had white hair and a black silk dress up

27

to her neck. She looked like the heroine of a play
by Victorien Sardou who had outlived the melo-
dramatic fury of her youth and now did crochet.
She was infinitely bored when you spoke to her of
Tolstoi or Chekov; but grew animated when she
talked of Jack London. She put a question to the
maiden lady which the maiden lady, though no
longer young, had no answer for.

"Why," she asked, "do you English write such
silly books about Russia?"

But then the first secretary of the British Legation appeared. He gave his entrance the significance of an event. He was very tall, baldish but
elegant, and he was beautifully dressed: he looked
with polite astonishment at the dazzling orders of
the Minister of Guatemala. The Chargé d'Affaires
of Montenegro, who flattered himself that he was
the best dressed man in the diplomatic body, but
was not quite sure whether the first secretary of
the British Legation thought him so, fluttered up
to him to ask his candid opinion of the frilled
shirt he wore. The Englishman placed a gold-
rimmed glass in his eye and looked at it for a moment gravely; then he paid the other a devastating
compliment. Everyone had come by now but the
wife of the French Military Attaché. They said
she was always late.

"*Elle est insupportable,*" said the handsome
wife of the Swiss banker.

But at last, magnificently indifferent to the fact
that she had kept everyone waiting for half an
hour, she swam into the room. She was tall on

her outrageously high heels, extremely thin, and
she wore a dress that gave you the impression
that she had nothing on at all. Her hair was
bobbed and blonde, and she was boldly painted.
She looked like a post-impressionist's idea of
patient Griselda. When she moved the air was
heavy with exotic odours. She gave the Minister
of Guatemala a jewelled, emaciated hand to kiss;
with a few smiling words made the banker's wife
feel passée, provincial, and portly; flung an im-
proper jest at the English lady whose embarrassment was mitigated by the knowledge that the wife
of the French Military Attaché was *très bien née;*
and drank three cocktails in rapid succession.

Dinner was served. The conversation varied
from a resonant, rolling French to a somewhat
halting English. They talked of this Minister
who had just written from Bucharest or Lima,
and that Counsellor's wife who found it so dull
in Christiania or so expensive in Washington. On
the whole it made little difference to them in what
capital they found themselves, for they did precisely the same things in Constantinople, Berne,
Stockholm and Peking. Entrenched within their
diplomatic privileges and supported by a lively
sense of their social consequence, they dwelt in a
world in which Copernicus had never existed, for
to them sun and stars circled obsequiously round
this earth of ours, and they were its centre. No
one knew why the English lady was there and
the wife of the Swiss director said privately that
she was without doubt a German spy. But she

was an authority on the country. She told you
that the Chinese had such perfect manners and
you really should have known the Empress
Dowager; she was a perfect darling. You knew
very well that in Constantinople she would have
assured you that the Turks were such perfect
gentlemen and the Sultana Fatima was a perfect
dear and spoke such wonderful French. Home-
less, she was at home wherever her country had a
diplomatic representative.

The first secretary of the British Legation
thought the party rather mixed. He spoke
French more like a Frenchman than any Frenchman who ever lived. He was a man of taste, and
he had a natural aptitude for being right. He
only knew the right people and only read the right
books; he admired none but the right music and
cared for none but the right pictures; he bought
his clothes at the right tailor's and his shirts from
the only possible haberdasher. You listened to
him with stupefaction. Presently you wished with
all your heart that he would confess to a liking
for something just a little vulgar: you would have
felt more at your ease if only with bold idiosyn-
crasy he had claimed that *The Soul's Awakening*
was a work of art or *The Rosary* a masterpiece.
But his taste was faultless. He was perfect and
you were half afraid that he knew it, for in repose
his face had the look of one who bears an intolerable burden. And then you discovered that he
wrote *vers libre*. You breathed again.

30

II: AT A TREATY PORT

There was about the party a splendour which has vanished from the dinner tables of England. The mahogany groaned with silver. In the middle of the snowy damask cloth was a centrepiece of yellow silk such as you were unwillingly constrained to buy in the bazaars of your prim youth and on this was a massive épergne. Tall silver vases in which were large chrysanthemums made it possible to catch only glimpses of the persons opposite you, and tall silver candlesticks reared their proud heads two by two down the length of the table. Each course was served with its appropriate wine, sherry with the soup and hock with the fish; and there were the two entrées, a white entrée and a brown entrée, which the careful housekeeper of the nineties felt were essential to a properly arranged dinner.

Perhaps the conversation was less varied than the courses, for guests and hosts had seen one another nearly every day for an intolerable number of years and each topic that arose was seized upon desperately only to be exhausted and followed by a formidable silence. They talked of racing and golf and shooting. They would have thought it bad form to touch upon the abstract and there were no politics for them to discuss. China bored them all, they did not want to speak of that; they only knew just so much about it as was necessary to their business, and they looked with distrust upon any man who studied the Chinese language. Why should he unless he were a missionary or a Chinese Secretary at the Legation? You could hire an interpreter for twenty-five dollars a month and it was well known that all those fellows who went in for Chinese grew queer in the head. They were all persons of consequence. There was number one at Jardine's with his wife, and the manager of the Hong-Kong and Shanghai Bank with his wife, the A. P. C. man and his wife, and the B. A. T. man with his wife, and the B. & S. man with his wife. They wore their evening clothes a little uneasily as though they wore them from a sense of duty to their country rather than as a comfortable change from day dress. They had come to the party because they had nothing else in the world to do, but when the moment came that they could decently take their leave they would go with a sigh of relief. They were bored to death with one another.

VII

THE ALTAR OF HEAVEN

IT stands open to the sky, three round terraces of white marble, placed one above the other, which are reached by four marble staircases, and these face the four points of the compass. It represents the celestial sphere with its cardinal points. A great park surrounds it and this again is surrounded by high walls. And hither, year after year, on the night of the winter solstice, for then heaven is reborn, generation after generation came the Son of Heaven solemnly to worship the original creator of his house. Escorted by princes and the great men of the realm, followed by his troops, the emperor purified by fasting proceeded to the altar. And here awaited him princes and ministers and mandarins, each in his allotted place, musicians and the dancers of the sacred dance. In the scanty light of the great torches the ceremonial robes were darkly splendid. And before the tablet on which were inscribed the words: Imperial Heaven—Supreme Emperor, he offered incense, jade, and silk, broth and rice spirit. He knelt and knocked his forehead against the marble pavement nine times.

And here at the very spot where the vice-regent

of heaven and earth knelt down, Willard B. Untermeyer wrote his name in a fine bold hand and the
town and state he came from, Hastings, Nebraska.
So he sought to attach his fleeting personality to
the recollection of that grandeur of which some
dim rumour had reached him. He thought that
so men would remember him when he was no more.
He aimed in this crude way at immortality. But
vain are the hopes of men. For no sooner had he
sauntered down the steps than a Chinese caretaker
who had been leaning against the balustrade, idly
looking at the blue sky, came forward, spat neatly
on the spot where Willard B. Untermeyer had
written, and with his foot smeared his spittle over
the name. In a moment no trace remained that
Willard B. Untermeyer had ever visited that place.

VIII

THE SERVANTS OF GOD

THEY were sitting side by side, two missionaries, talking to one another of perfectly trivial things, in the way people talk who wish to show each other civility but have nothing in common; and they would have been surprised to be told that they had certainly one admirable thing in common, goodness, for both had this also in common, humility; though perhaps in the Englishman it was more deliberate, and so, if more conspicuous less natural, than it was in the Frenchman. Otherwise the contrasts between them were almost ludicrous. The Frenchman was hard on eighty, a tall man, still unbent; and his large bones suggested that in youth he had been a man of uncommon strength. Now his only sign of power lay in his eyes, immensely large so that you could not help noticing their strange expression, and flashing. That is an epithet often applied to eyes, but I do not think I have ever seen any to which it might be applied so fitly. There was really a flame in them and they seemed to emit light. They had a wildness which hardly suggested sanity. They were the eyes of a prophet in Israel. His nose was large and aggressive, his chin was firm and square. At no time could he have been a man to trifle with, but in his prime he must have been terrific. Perhaps the passion of his eyes bespoke battles long fought out in the uttermost depths of his heart, and his soul cried out in them, vanquished and bleeding, yet triumphant, and he exulted in the unclosed wound which he offered in willing sacrifice to Almighty God. He felt the cold in his old bones and he wore wrapped about him like a soldier's cloak a great fur and on his head a cap of Chinese sable. He was a magnificent figure. He had been in China for half a century and thrice he had fled for his life when the Chinese had attacked his mission.

"I trust they won't attack it again," he said, smiling, "for I am too old now to make these precipitate journeys." He shrugged his shoulders: "*Je serai martyr.*"

He lit a long black cigar and puffed it with great enjoyment.

The other was very much younger, he could not have been more than fifty, and he had not been in China for more than twenty years. He was a member of the English Church Mission and he was dressed in a grey tweed suit and a spotted tie. He sought to look as little like a clergyman as possible. He was a little taller than the average, but he was so fat that he looked stumpy. He had a round good-natured face, with red cheeks and a grey moustache of the variety known as toothbrush. He was very bald, but with a pardonable and touching vanity he had grown his hair long

enough on one side to be brought over the scalp
and so give himself at all events the illusion that
his head was well-covered. He was a jovial fellow,
with a hearty laugh, and it rang out loudly, honest
and true, when he chaffed his friends or was
chaffed by them. He had the humour of a school-
boy and you could imagine him shaking in all his
bulk when someone slipped on a piece of orange
peel. But the laughter would be stopped, and he
would redden, as it struck him suddenly that the
man who slipped might have hurt himself, and
then he would be all kindness and sympathy. For
it was impossible to be with him for ten minutes
without realising the tenderness of his heart. You
felt that it would be impossible to ask him to do
anything he would not gladly do, and if perhaps
at first his heartiness would make it difficult to
go to him in your spiritual needs you could be
sure in all practical affairs of his attention, sympathy, and good sense. He was a man whose purse
was always open to the indigent and whose time
was always at the service of those who wanted it.
And yet perhaps it is unjust to say that in the
affairs of the soul his help would not be very
effectual, for though he could not speak to you,
like the old Frenchman, with the authority of a
church that has never admitted doubt or with the
compelling fire of the ascetic, he would share your
distress with such a candid sympathy, consoling
you with his own hesitations, less a minister of
God then than a halting, tremulous man of the
same flesh as yourself, who sought to share with

you the hope and the consolation with which his own soul was refreshed, that perhaps in his own way he had something as good to offer as the other.

His story was a little unusual. He had been a soldier and he was pleased to talk of the old days when he had hunted with the Quorn and danced through the London season. He had no unhealthy feeling of past sin.

"I was a great dancer in my young days," he said, "but I expect I should be quite out of it now with all these new dances."

It was a good life so long as it lasted and though he did not for a moment regret it, he had no feeling of resentment for it. The call had come when he was in India. He did not exactly know how or why, it had just come, a sudden feeling that he must give up his life to bringing the heathen to the belief in Christ, but it was a feeling that he could not resist; it gave him no peace. He was a happy man now, enjoying his work.

"It's a slow business," he said, "but I see signs of progress and I love the Chinese. I wouldn't change my life here for any in the world."

The two missionaries said good-bye to one another.

"When are you going home?" asked the Englishman.

"*Moi?* Oh, in a day or two."

"I may not see you again then. I expect to go home in March."

But one meant the little town with its narrow

THE SERVANTS OF GOD

streets where he had lived for fifty years, since
when he left France, a young man, he left it for
ever; but the other meant the Elizabethan house
in Cheshire, with its smooth lawns and its oak
trees, where his ancestors had dwelt for three
centuries.

IX

THE INN

IT seems long since the night fell, and for an hour a coolie has walked before your chair carrying a lantern. It throws a thin circle of light in front of you, and as you pass you catch a pale glimpse (like a thing of beauty emerging vaguely from the ceaseless flux of common life) of a bamboo thicket, a flash of water in a rice field, or the heavy darkness of a banyan. Now and then a belated peasant bearing two heavy baskets on his yoke sidles by. The bearers walk more slowly, but after the long day they have lost none of their spirit, and they chatter gaily; they laugh, and one of them breaks into a fragment of tuneless song. But the causeway rises and the lantern throws its light suddenly on a whitewashed wall: you have reached the first miserable houses that straggle along the path outside the city wall, and two or three minutes more bring you to a steep flight of steps. The bearers take them at a run. You pass through the city gates. The narrow streets are multitudinous and in the shops they are busy still. The bearers shout raucously. The crowd divides and you pass through a double hedge of serried

curious people. Their faces are impassive and
their dark eyes stare mysteriously. The bearers,
their day's work done, march with a swinging
stride. Suddenly they stop, wheel to the right,
into a courtyard, and you have reached the inn.
Your chair is set down.

The inn—it consists of a long yard, partly
covered, with rooms opening on it on each side—
is lit by three or four oil lamps. They throw a
dim light immediately around them, but make the
surrounding darkness more impenetrable. All the
front of the yard is crowded with tables and at
these people are packed, eating rice or drinking
tea. Some of them play games you do not know.
At the great stove, where water in a cauldron is
perpetually heating and rice in a huge pan being
prepared, stand the persons of the inn. They
serve out rapidly great bowls of rice and fill the
teapots which are incessantly brought them.
Further back a couple of naked coolies, sturdy,
thickset and supple, are sluicing themselves with
boiling water. You walk to the end of the yard
where, facing the entrance but protected from the
vulgar gaze by a screen, is the principal guest
chamber.

It is a spacious, windowless room, with a floor
of trodden earth, lofty, for it goes the whole
height of the inn, with an open roof. The walls
are whitewashed, showing the beams, so that they
remind you of a farmhouse in Sussex. The furniture consists of a square table, with a couple of
straight-backed wooden arm-chairs, and three or

41

four wooden pallets covered with matting on the least dirty of which you will presently lay your bed. In a cup of oil a taper gives a tiny point of light. They bring you your lantern and you wait while your dinner is cooked. The bearers are merry now that they have set down their loads. They wash their feet and put on clean sandals and smoke their long pipes.

How precious then is the inordinate length of your book (for you are travelling light and you have limited yourself to three) and how jealously you read every word of every page so that you may delay as long as possible the dreaded moment when you must reach the end! You are mightily thankful then to the authors of long books and when you turn over their pages, reckoning how long you can make them last, you wish they were half as long again. You do not ask then for the perfect lucidity which he who runs may read. A complicated phraseology which makes it needful to read the sentence a second time to get its meaning is not unwelcome; a profusion of metaphor, giving your fancy ample play, a richness of allusion affording you the delight of recognition, are then qualities beyond price. Then if the thought is elaborate without being profound (for you have been on the road since dawn and of the forty miles of the day's journey you have footed it more than half) you have the perfect book for the occasion.

But the noise in the inn suddenly increases to a din and looking out you see that more travellers,

a party of Chinese in sedan chairs, have arrived.
They take the rooms on each side of you and
through the thin walls you hear their loud talking
far into the night. With a lazy, restful eye, your
whole body conscious of the enjoyment of lying
in bed, taking a sensual pleasure in its fatigue,
you follow the elaborate pattern of the transom.
The dim lamp in the yard shines through the torn
paper with which it is covered, and its intricate
design is black against the light. At last everything is quiet but for a man in the next room who
is coughing painfully. It is the peculiar, repeated
cough of phthisis, and hearing it at intervals
through the night you wonder how long the poor
devil can live. You rejoice in your own rude
strength. Then a cock crows loudly, just behind
your head, it seems; and not far away a bugler
blows a long blast on his bugle, a melancholy
wail; the inn begins to stir again; lights are lit,
and the coolies make ready their loads for another
day.

X

THE GLORY HOLE

IT is a sort of little cubicle in a corner of the chandler's store just under the ceiling and you reach it by a stair which is like a ship's companion. It is partitioned off from the shop by matchboarding, about four feet high, so that when you sit on the wooden benches that surround the table you can see into the shop with all its stores. Here are coils of rope, oilskins, heavy sea-boots, hurricane lamps, hams, tinned goods, liquor of all sorts, curios to take home to your wife and children, clothes, I know not what. There is everything that a foreign ship can want in an Eastern port. You can watch the Chinese, salesmen and customers, and they have a pleasantly mysterious air as though they were concerned in nefarious business. You can see who comes into the shop and since it is certainly a friend bid him join you in the Glory Hole. Through the wide doorway you see the sun beating down on the stone pavement of the roadway and the coolies scurrying past with their heavy loads. At about midday the company begins to assemble, two or three pilots, Captain Thompson and Captain Brown, old men who have sailed the China Seas

44

for thirty years and now have a comfortable billet ashore, the skipper of a tramp from Shanghai, and the taipans of one or two tea firms. The boy stands silently waiting for orders and he brings the drinks and the dice-box. Talk flows rather prosily at first. A boat was wrecked the other day going in to Foochow, that fellow Maclean, the engineer of the An-Chan has made a pot of money in rubber lately, the consul's wife is coming out from home in the *Empress*; but by the time the dice-box has travelled round the table and the loser has signed the chit, the glasses are empty and the dice-box is reached for once more. The boy brings the second round of drinks. Then the tongues of these stolid, stubborn men are loosened a little and they begin to talk of the past. One of the pilots knew the port first hard on fifty years ago. Ah, those were the great days.

"That's when you ought to have seen the Glory Hole," he says, with a smile.

Those were the days of the tea clippers, when there would be thirty or forty ships in the harbour, waiting for their cargo. Everyone had plenty of money to spend then, and the Glory Hole was the centre of life in the port. If you wanted to find a man, why, you came to the Glory Hole, and if he wasn't there he'd be sure to come along soon. The agents did their business with the skippers there, and the doctor didn't have office hours; he went to the Glory Hole at noon and if anyone was sick he attended to him there

and then. Those were the days when men knew
how to drink. They would come at midday and
drink all through the afternoon, a boy bringing
them a bite if they were hungry, and drink all
through the night. Fortunes were lost and won
in the Glory Hole, for they were gamblers then
and a man would risk all the profits of his run in
a game of cards. Those were the good old days.
But now the trade was gone, the tea clippers no
longer thronged the harbour, the port was dead,
and the young men, the young men of the A. P. C.
or of Jardine's, turned up their noses at the
Glory Hole. And as the old pilot talked that
dingy little cubicle with its stained table seemed
to be for a moment peopled with those old skippers, hardy, reckless, and adventurous, of a day
that has gone for ever.

XI

FEAR

I WAS staying a night with him on the road.
The mission stood on a little hill just outside the gates of a populous city. The first
thing I noticed about him was the difference
of his taste. The missionary's house as a rule is
furnished in a style which is almost an outrage
to decency. The parlour, with its air of an unused room, is papered with a gaudy paper, and
on the wall hang texts, engravings of sentimental
pictures—*The Soul's Awakening* and Luke Filde's
The Doctor—or, if the missionary has been long
in the country, congratulatory scrolls on stiff
red paper. There is a Brussels carpet on the
floor, rocking chairs if the household is American
and a stiff arm-chair on each side of the fireplace
if it is English. There is a sofa which is so placed
that nobody sits on it and by the grim look of
it few can want to. There are lace curtains on
the windows. Here and there are occasional tables
on which are photographs and what-nots with
modern porcelain on them. The dining-room has
an appearance of more use, but almost the whole
of it is taken up by a large table and when you
sit at it you are crowded into the fireplace. But

in Mr. Wingrove's study there were books from floor to ceiling, a table littered with papers, curtains of a rich green stuff, and over the fireplace a Tibetan bannner. There was a row of Tibetan Buddhas on the chimney piece.

"I don't know how it is, but you've got just the feeling of college rooms about the place," I said.

"Do you think so?" he answered. "I was a tutor at Oriel for some time."

He was a man of nearly fifty, I should think, tall·and well-covered through not stout, with grey hair cut very short and a reddish face. One imagined that he must be a jovial man fond of laughter, an easy talker and a good fellow; but his eyes disconcerted you: they were grave and unsmiling; they had a look that I could only describe as harassed. I wondered if I had fallen upon him at an inconvenient moment when his mind was taken up with irksome matters, yet somehow I felt that this was not a passing expression, but a settled one rather, and I could not understand it. He had just that look of anxiety which you see in certain forms of heart disease. He chatted about one thing and another, then he said:

"I hear my wife come in. Shall we go into the drawing-room?"

He led me in and introduced me to a little thin woman, with gold-rimmed spectacles and a shy manner. It was plain that she belonged to a different class from her husband. The missionaries for the most part with all manner of virtues have not those which we can find no better way to de-

scribe than under the category of good breeding.
They may be saints but they are not often gentlemen. Now it struck me that Mr. Wingrove
was a gentleman, for it was evident that his wife
was not a lady. She had a vulgar intonation.
The drawing-room was furnished in a way I had
never before seen in a missionary's house. There
was a Chinese carpet on the floor. Chinese pictures, old ones, hung on the yellow walls. Two
or three Ming tiles gave a dash of colour. In the
middle of the room was a blackwood table, elabor-
ately carved, and on it was a figure in white porcelain. I made a trivial remark.

"I don't much care for all these Chinese things
meself," answered my hostess briskly, "but Mr.
Wingrove's set on them. I'd clear them all out if
I had my way."

I laughed, not because I was amused, and then
I caught in Mr. Wingrove's eyes a flash of icy
hatred. I was astonished. But it passed in a
moment.

"We won't have them if you don't like them, my
dear," he said gently. "They can be put away."

"Oh, I don't mind them if they please you."

We began to talk about my journey and in
the course of conversation I happened to ask Mr.
Wingrove how long it was since he had been in
England.

"Seventeen years," he said.

I was surprised.

"But I thought you had one year's furlough
every seven?"

"Yes, but I haven't cared to go."

"Mr. Wingrove thinks it's bad for the work to go away for a year like that," explained his wife. "Of course I don't care to go without him."

I wondered how it was that he had ever come to China. The actual details of the call fascinate me, and often enough you find people who are willing to talk of it, though you have to form your own opinion on the matter less from the words they say than from the implications of them; but I did not feel that Mr. Wingrove was a man who would be induced either directly or indirectly to speak of that intimate experience. He evidently took his work very seriously.

"Are there other foreigners here?" I asked.

"No."

"It must be very lonely," I said.

"I think I prefer it so," he answered, looking at one of the pictures on the wall. "They'd only be business people, and you know"—he smiled—"they haven't much use for missionaries. And they're not so intellectual that it is a great hardship to be deprived of their company.

"And of course we're not really alone, you know," said Mrs. Wingrove. "We have two evangelists and then there are two young ladies who teach. And there are the school children."

Tea was brought in and we gossiped desultorily. Mr. Wingrove seemed to speak with effort, and I had increasingly that feeling in him of perturbed repression. He had pleasing manners and was certainly trying to be cordial and yet I had

50

a sense of effort. I led the conversation to Oxford, mentioning various friends whom he might know, but he gave me no encouragement.

"It's so long since I left home," he said, "and I haven't kept up with anyone. There's a great deal of work in a mission like this and it absorbs one entirely."

I thought he was exaggerating a little, so I remarked:

"Well, by the number of books you have I take it that you get a certain amount of time for reading."

"I very seldom read," he answered with abruptness, in a voice that I knew already was not quite his own.

I was puzzled. There was something odd about the man. At last, as was inevitable, I suppose, he began to talk of the Chinese. Mrs. Wingrove said the same things about them that I had already heard so many missionaries say. They were a lying people, untrustworthy, cruel, and dirty, but a faint light was visible in the East; though the results of missionary endeavour were not very noteworthy as yet, the future was promising. They no longer believed in their old gods and the power of the literati was broken. It is an attitude of mistrust and dislike tempered by optimism. But Mr. Wingrove mitigated his wife's strictures. He dwelt on the good-nature of the Chinese, on their devotion to their parents and on their love for their children.

"Mr. Wingrove won't hear a word against the Chinese," said his wife, "he simply loves them."

"I think they have great qualities," he said. "You can't walk through those crowded streets of theirs without having that impressed on you."

"I don't believe Mr. Wingrove notices the smells," his wife laughed.

At that moment there was a knock at the door and a young woman came in. She had the long skirts and the unbound feet of the native Christian, and on her face a look that was at once cringing and sullen. She said something to Mrs. Wingrove. I happened to catch sight of Mr. Wingrove's face. When he saw her there passed over it an expression of the most intense physical repulsion, it was distorted as though by an odour that nauseated him, and then immediately it vanished and his lips twitched to a pleasant smile; but the effort was too great and he showed only a tortured grimace. I looked at him with amazement. Mrs. Wingrove with an "excuse me" got up and left the room.

"That is one of our teachers," said Mr. Wingrove in that same set voice which had a little puzzled me before. "She's invaluable. I put infinite reliance on her. She has a very fine character."

Then, I hardly know why, in a flash I saw the truth; I saw the disgust in his soul for all that his will loved. I was filled with the excitement which an explorer may feel when after a hazardous journey he comes upon a country with features

new and unexpected. Those tortured eyes explained themselves, the unnatural voice, the measured restraint with which he praised, that air he
had of a hunted man. Notwithstanding all he
said he hated the Chinese with a hatred beside
which his wife's distaste was insignificant. When
he walked through the teeming streets of the city
it was an agony to him, his missionary life revolted him, his soul was like the raw shoulders
of the coolies and the carrying pole burnt the
bleeding wound. He would not go home because
he could not bear to see again what he cared for
so much, he would not read his books because they
reminded him of the life he loved so passionately,
and perhaps he had married that vulgar wife in
order to cut himself off more resolutely from a
world that his every instinct craved for. He
martyred his tortured soul with a passionate exasperation.

I tried to see how the call had come. I think
that for years he had been completely happy in
his easy ways at Oxford; and he had loved his
work, with its pleasant companionship, his books,
his holidays in France and Italy. He was a contented man and asked nothing better than to spend
the rest of his days in just such a fashion; but I
know not what obscure feeling had gradually
taken hold of him that his life was too lazy, too
contented; I think he was always a religious man
and perhaps some early belief, instilled into him
in childhood and long forgotten, of a jealous God
who hated his creatures to be happy on earth,

rankled in the depths of his heart; I think because he was so well satisfied with his life he began to think it was sinful. A restless anxiety seized him. Whatever he thought with his intelligence his instincts began to tremble with the dread of eternal punishment. I do not know what put the idea of China into his head, but at first he must have thrust it aside with violent repulsion; and perhaps the very violence of his repulsion impressed the idea on him, for he found it haunting him. I think he said that he would not go, but I think he felt that he would have to. God was pursuing him and wherever he hid himself God followed. With his reason he struggled, but with his heart he was caught. He could not help himself. At least he gave in.

I knew I should never see him again and I had not the time to spend on the commonplaces of conversation before a reasonable familiarity would permit me to talk of more intimate matters. I seized the opportunity while we were still alone.

"Tell me," I said, "do you believe God will condemn the Chinese to eternal punishment if they don't accept Christianity?"

I am sure my question was crude and tactless, for the old man in him tightened his lips. But nevertheless he answered.

"The whole teaching of the gospel forces one to that conclusion. There is not a single argument which people have adduced to the contrary which has the force of the plain words of Jesus Christ."

XII

THE PICTURE

I DO not know whether he was a mandarin bound for the capital of the province, or some student travelling to a seat of learning, nor what the reason that delayed him in the most miserable of all the miserable inns in China. Perhaps one or other of his bearers, hidden somewhere to smoke a pipe of opium (for it is cheap in that neighborhood and you must be prepared for trouble with your coolies) could not be found. Perhaps a storm of torrential rain had held him for an hour an unwilling prisoner.

The room was so low that you could easily touch the rafters with your hand. The mud walls were covered with dirty whitewash, here and there worn away, and all round on wooden pallets were straw beds for the coolies who were the inn's habitual guests. The sun alone enabled you to support the melancholy squalor. It shone through the latticed window, a beam of golden light, and threw on the trodden earth of the floor a pattern of an intricate and splendid richness.

And here to pass an idle moment he had taken his stone tablet and mixing a little water with the stick of ink which he rubbed on it, seized the fine brush with which he executed the beautiful characters of the Chinese writing (he was surely proud of his exquisite calligraphy and it was a welcome gift which he made his friends when he sent them a scroll on which was written a maxim, glitteringly compact, of the divine Confucius) and with a bold hand he drew on the wall a branch of plum-blossom and a bird perched on it. It was done very lightly, but with an admirable ease; I know not what happy chance guided the artist's touch, for the bird was all a-quiver with life and the plum-blossoms were tremulous on their stalks. The soft airs of spring blew through the sketch into that sordid chamber, and for the beating of a pulse you were in touch with the Eternal.

XIII

HER BRITANNIC MAJESTY'S
REPRESENTATIVE

H
E was a man of less than middle height, with stiff brown hair *en brosse*, a little toothbrush moustache, and glasses through which his blue eyes, looking at you aggressively, were somewhat distorted. There was a defiant perkiness in his appearance which reminded you of the cock-sparrow, and as he asked you to sit down and inquired your business, meanwhile sorting the papers littered on his desk as though you had disturbed him in the midst of important affairs, you had the feeling that he was on the look out for an opportunity to put you in your place. He had cultivated the official manner to perfection. You were the public, an unavoidable nuisance, and the only justification for your existence was that you did what you were told without argument or delay. But even officials have their weakness and somehow it chanced that he found it very difficult to bring any business to an end without confiding his grievance to you. It appeared that people, missionaries especially, thought him supercilious and domineering. He assured you that he thought there was a

great deal of good in missionaries; it is true that
many of them were ignorant and unreasonable,
and he didn't like their attitude; in his district
most of them were Canadians, and personally he
didn't like Canadians; but as for saying that he
put on airs of superiority (he fixed his pince-nez
more firmly on his nose) it was monstrously un-
true. On the contrary he went out of his way to
help them, but it was only natural that he should
help them in his way rather than in theirs. It
was hard to listen to him without a smile, for in
every word he said you felt how exasperating he
must be to the unfortunate persons over whom he
had control. His manner was deplorable. He had
developed the gift of putting up your back to a
degree which is very seldom met with. He was
in short a vain, irritable, bumptious, and tiresome
little man.

During the revolution, while a lot of firing was
going on in the city between the rival factions,
he had occasion to go to the Southern general on
official business connected with the safety of his
nationals, and on his way through the yamen he
came across three prisoners being led out to execu-
tion. He stopped the officer in charge of the firing
party and finding out what was about to happen
vehemently protested. These were prisoners of
war and it was barbarity to kill them. The officer
—very rudely, in the consul's words—told him
that he must carry out his orders. The consul fired
up. He wasn't going to let a confounded Chinese
officer talk to him in that way. An altercation

ensued. The general informed of what was oc-
curring sent out to ask the consul to come in to
him, but the consul refused to move till the prisoners, three wretched coolies green with fear, were
handed over to his safe-keeping. The officer waved
him aside and ordered his firing squad to take aim.
Then the consul—I can see him fixing his glasses
on his nose and his hair bristling fiercely—then the
consul stepped forwards between the levelled rifles
and the three miserable men, and told the soldiers
to shoot and be damned. There was hesitation and
confusion. It was plain that the rebels did not
want to shoot a British consul. I suppose there
was a hurried consultation. The three prisoners
were given over to him and in triumph the little
man marched back to the consulate.

"Damn it, Sir," he said furiously, "I almost
thought the blighters would have the confounded
cheek to shoot me."

They are strange people the British. If their
manners were as good as their courage is great
they would merit the opinion they have of themselves.

XIV

THE OPIUM DEN

ON the stage it makes a very effective set. It is dimly lit. The room is low and squalid. In one corner a lamp burns mysteriously before a hideous image and incense fills the theatre with its exotic scent. A pig-tailed Chinaman wanders to and fro, aloof and saturnine, while on wretched pallets lie stupefied the victims of the drug. Now and then one of them breaks into frantic raving. There is a highly dramatic scene where some poor creature, unable to pay for the satisfaction of his craving, with prayers and curses begs the villainous proprietor for a pipe to still his anguish. I have read also in novels descriptions which made my blood run cold. And when I was taken to an opium den by a smooth-spoken Eurasian the narrow, winding stairway up which he led me prepared me sufficiently to receive the thrill I expected. I was introduced into a neat enough room, brightly lit, divided into cubicles the raised floor of which, covered with clean matting, formed a convenient couch. In one an elderly gentleman, with a grey head and very beautiful hands, was quietly reading a newspaper, with his long pipe by his side. In another two coolies were lying, with a pipe between them, which they alternately prepared and smoked. They were young men, of a hearty appearance, and they smiled at me in a friendly way. One of them offered me a smoke. In a third four men squatted over a chess-board, and a little further on a man was dandling a baby (the inscrutable Oriental has a passion for children) while the baby's mother, whom I took to be the landlord's wife, a plump, pleasant-faced woman, watched him with a broad smile on her lips. It was a cheerful spot, comfortable, home-like, and cosy. It reminded me somewhat of the little intimate beer-houses of Berlin where the tired working man could go in the evening and spend a peaceful hour. Fiction is stranger than fact.

XV

THE LAST CHANCE

IT was pathetically obvious that she had come to China to be married, and what made it almost tragic was that not a single man in the treaty port was ignorant of the fact. She was a big woman with an ungainly figure; her hands and feet were large; she had a large nose, indeed all her features were large; but her blue eyes were fine. She was perhaps a little too conscious of them. She was a blonde and she was thirty. In the daytime when she wore sensible boots, a short skirt, and a slouch hat, she was personable; but in the evening, in blue silk to enhance the colour of her eyes, in a frock cut by heaven knows what suburban dressmaker from the models in an illustrated paper, when she set herself out to be alluring she was an object that made you horribly ill-at-ease. She wished to be all things to all unmarried men. She listened brightly while one of them talked of shooting and she listened gaily when another talked of the freight on tea. She clapped her hands with girlish excitement when they discussed the races which were to be run next week. She was desperately fond of dancing, with a young American, and she made him promise to take her to a baseball match; but dancing wasn't the only thing she cared for (you can have too much of a good thing) and, with the elderly, but single, taipan of an important firm, what she simply loved was a game of golf. She was willing to be taught billiards by a young man who had lost his leg in the war and she gave her sprightly attention to the manager of a bank who told her what he thought of silver. She was not much interested in the Chinese, for that was a subject which was not very good form in the circles in which she found herself, but being a woman she could not help being revolted at the way in which Chinese women were treated.

"You know, they don't have a word to say about who they're going to marry," she explained. "It's all arranged by go-betweens and the man doesn't even see the girl till he's married her. There's no romance or anything like that. And as far as love goes . . ."

Words failed her. She was a thoroughly good-natured creature. She would have made any of those men, young or old, a perfectly good wife. And she knew it.

XVI

THE NUN

THE convent lay white and cool among the trees on the top of a hill; and as I stood at the gateway, waiting to be let in, I looked down at the tawny river glittering in the sunlight and at the rugged mountains beyond. It was the Mother Superior who received me, a placid, sweet-faced lady with a soft voice and an accent which told me that she came from the South of France. She showed me the orphans who were in her charge, busy at the lace-making which the nuns had taught them, smiling shyly; and she showed me the hospital where lay soldiers suffering from dysentery, typhoid, and malaria. They were squalid and dirty. The Mother Superior told me she was a Basque. The mountains that she looked out on from the convent windows reminded her of the Pyrenees. She had been in China for twenty years. She said that it was hard sometimes never to see the sea; here on the great river they were a thousand miles away from it; and because I knew the country where she was born she talked to me a little of the fine roads that led over the mountains—ah, they did not have them here in China—and the vineyards and

64

the pleasant villages with their running streams
that nestled at the foot of the hills. But the
Chinese were good people. The orphans were very
quick with their fingers and they were industrious;
the Chinese sought them as wives because they had
learnt useful things in the convent, and even after
they were married they could earn a little money
by their needles. And the soldiers too, they were
not so bad as people said; after all *les pauvres
petits*, they did not want to be soldiers; they would
much sooner be at home working in the fields.
Those whom the sisters had nursed through illness
were not devoid of gratitude. Sometimes when
they were coming along in a chair and overtook
two nuns who had been in the town to buy things
and were laden with parcels, they would offer to
take their parcels in the chair. *Au fond*, they
were not bad hearted.

"They do not go so far as to get out and let
the nuns ride in their stead?" I asked.

"A nun in their eyes is only a woman," she
smiled indulgently. "You must not ask from people more than they are capable of giving."

How true, and yet how hard to remember!

XVII

HENDERSON

IT was very hard to look at him without a chuckle, for his appearance immediately told you all about him. When you saw him at the club, reading *The London Mercury* or lounging at the bar with a gin and bitters at his elbow (no cocktails for him) his unconventionality attracted your attention; but you recognised him at once, for he was a perfect specimen of his class. His unconventionality was exquisitely conventional. Everything about him was according to standard, from his square-toed, serviceable boots to his rather long, untidy hair. He wore a loose low collar that showed a thick neck and loose, somewhat shabby but well-cut clothes. He always smoked a short briar pipe. He was very humorous on the subject of cigarettes. He was a biggish fellow, athletic, with fine eyes and a pleasant voice. He talked fluently. His language was often obscene, not because his mind was impure, but because his bent was democratic. As you guessed by the look of him he drank beer (not in fact but in the spirit) with Mr. Chesterton and walked the Sussex downs with Mr. Hilaire Belloc. He had played football at Oxford, but with Mr. Wells

he despised the ancient seat of learning. He
looked upon Mr. Bernard Shaw as a little out
of date, but he had still great hopes of Mr. Gran-
ville Barker. He had had many serious talks with
Mr. and Mrs. Sydney Webb, and he was a member
of the Fabian Society. The only point where he
touched upon the same world as the frivolous was
his appreciation of the Russian Ballet. He wrote
rugged poems about prostitutes, dogs, lamp-posts,
Magdalen College, public houses and country
vicarages. He held English, French, and Americans in scorn; but on the other hand (he was no
misanthropist) he would not listen to a word in
dispraise of Tamils, Bengalis, Kaffirs, Germans, or
Greeks. At the club they thought him rather a
wild fellow.

"A socialist, you know," they said.

But he was junior partner in a well-known and
respectable firm, and one of the peculiarities of
China is that your position excuses your idiosyncrasies. It may be notorious that you beat your
wife, but if you are manager of a well-established
bank the world will be civil to you and ask you to
dinner. So when Henderson announced his social-
istic opinions they merely laughed. When he
first came to Shanghai he refused to use the
jinrickshaw. It revolted his sense of personal
dignity that a man, a human being no different
from himself, should drag him hither and thither.
So he walked. He swore it was good exercise and
it kept him fit; besides, it gave him a thirst he
wouldn't sell for twenty dollars, and he drank his

beer with gusto. But Shanghai is very hot and sometimes he was in a hurry so now and again he was obliged to use the degrading vehicle. It made him feel uncomfortable, but it was certainly convenient. Presently he came to use it frequently, but he always thought of the boy between the shafts as a man and a brother.

He had been three years in Shanghai when I saw him. We had spent the morning in the Chinese city, going from shop to shop and our rickshaw boys were hot with sweat; every minute or two they wiped their foreheads with ragged handkerchiefs. We were bound now for the club and had nearly reached it when Henderson remembered that he wanted to get Mr. Bertrand Russell's new book, which had just reached Shanghai. He stopped the boys and told them to go back.

"Don't you think we might leave it till after luncheon?" I said. "Those fellows are sweating like pigs."

"It's good for them," he answered. "You mustn't ever pay attention to the Chinese. You see, we're only here because they fear us. We're the ruling race."

I did not say anything. I did not even smile.

"The Chinese always have had masters and they always will."

A passing car separated us for a moment and when he came once more abreast of me he had put the matter aside.

"You men who live in England don't know what it means to us when new books get out here," he

68

remarked. "I read everything that Bertrand Russell writes. Have you seen the last one?

"Roads to Freedom? Yes. I read it before I left England."

"I've read several reviews. I think he's got hold of some interesting ideas."

I think Henderson was going to enlarge on them, but the rickshaw boy passed the turning he should have taken.

"Round the corner, you bloody fool," cried Henderson, and to emphasize his meaning he gave the man a smart kick on the bottom.

XVIII

DAWN

IT is night still and the courtyard of the
inn is rich with deep patches of darkness.
Lanterns throw fitful lights on the coolies
busily preparing their loads for the journey.
They shout and laugh, angrily argue with one
another, and vociferously quarrel. I go out into
the street and walk along preceded by a boy with
a lantern. Here and there behind closed doors
cocks are crowing. But in many of the shops the
shutters are down already and the indefatigable
people are beginning their long day. Here an
apprentice is sweeping the floor, and there a man
is washing his hands and face. A wick burning
in a cup of oil is all his light. I pass a tavern
where half a dozen persons are seated at an early
meal. The ward gate is closed, but a watchman
lets me through a postern and I walk along a wall
by a sluggish stream in which are reflected the
bright stars. Then I reach the great gate of the
city, and this time one half of it is open; I pass
out, and there, awaiting me, all ghostly, is the
dawn. The day and the long road and the open
country lie before me.

Put out the lantern. Behind me the darkness

pales to a mist of purple and I know that soon this will kindle to a rosy flush. I can make out the causeway well enough and the water in the padi fields reflects already a wan and shadowy light. It is no longer night, but it is not yet day. This is the moment of most magical beauty, when the hills and the valleys, the trees and the water, have a mystery which is not of earth. For when once the sun has risen, for a time the world is very cheerless, the light is cold and grey like the light in a painter's studio, and there are no shadows to diaper the ground with a coloured pattern. Skirting the brow of a wooded hill I look down on the padi fields. But to call them fields is too grandiose. They are for the most part crescent shaped patches built on the slope of a hill, one below the other, so that they can be flooded. Firs and bamboos grow in the hollows as though placed there by a skilful gardener with a sense of ordered beauty to imitate formally the abandon of nature. In this moment of enchantment you do not look upon the scene of humble toil, but on the pleasure gardens of an emperor. Here throwing aside the cares of state, he might come in yellow silk embroidered with dragons, with jewelled bracelets on his wrists, to sport with a concubine so beautiful that men in after ages felt it natural if a dynasty was destroyed for her sake.

And now with the increasing day a mist arises from the padi fields and climbs half way up the gentle hills. You may see a hundred pictures of the sight before you, for it is one that the old

masters of China loved exceedingly. The little
hills, wooded to their summit, with a line of fir
trees along the crest, a firm silhouette against the
sky, the little hills rise behind one another, and
the varying level of the mist, forming a pattern,
gives the composition a completeness which yet
allows the imagination ample scope. The bamboos
grow right down to the causeway, their thin leaves
shivering in the shadow of a breeze, and they grow
with a high-bred grace so that they look like
groups of ladies in the Great Ming dynasty resting languidly by the way-side. They have been
to some temple, and their silken dresses are richly
wrought with flowers and in their hair are precious
ornaments of jade. They rest there for a while
on their small feet, their golden lilies, gossiping
elegantly, for do they not know that the best use
of culture is to talk nonsense with distinction; and
in a moment slipping back into their chairs they
will be gone. But the road turns and my God,
the bamboos, the Chinese bamboos, transformed
by some magic of the mist, look just like the hops
of a Kentish field. Do you remember the sweet
smelling hop-fields and the fat green meadows,
the railway line that runs along the sea and the
long shining beach and the desolate greyness of
the English Channel? The seagull flies over the
wintry coldness and the melancholy of its cry is
almost unbearable.

XIX

THE POINT OF HONOUR

NOTHING hinders friendly relations between different countries so much as the fantastic notions which they cherish about one another's characteristics, and perhaps no nation has suffered so much from the misconception of its neighbours as the French. They have been considered a frivolous race, incapable of profound thought, flippant, immoral, and unreliable. Even the virtues that have been allowed them, their brilliancy, their gaiety, have been allowed them (at least by the English) in a patronising way; for they were not virtues on which the Anglo-Saxon set great store. It was never realised that there is a deep seriousness at the bottom of the French character and that the predominant concern of the average Frenchman is the concern for his personal dignity. It is by no hazard that La Rochefoucauld, a keen judge of human nature in general and of his countrymen in particular, should have made *l'honneur* the pivot of his system. The punctiliousness with which our neighbours regard it has often entertained the Briton who is accustomed to look upon himself with humour; but it is a living force, as the phrase goes, with the Frenchman, and you cannot hope to understand him unless you bear in mind always the susceptibility of his sense of honour.

These reflections were suggested to me whenever I saw the Vicomte de Steenvoorde driving in his sumptuous car or seated at the head of his own table. He represented certain important French interests in China and was said to have more power at the Quai d'Orsay than the minister himself. There was never a very cordial feeling between the pair, since the latter not unnaturally resented that one of his nationals should deal in diplomatic matters with the Chinese behind his back. The esteem in which M. de Steenvoorde was held at home was sufficiently proved by the red button that adorned the lappet of his frock coat.

The Vicomte had a fine head, somewhat bald, but not unbecomingly (*une légère calvitie*, as the French novelists put it and thereby rob the cruel fact of half its sting) a nose like the great Duke of Wellington's, bright black eyes under heavy eyelids, and a small mouth hidden by an exceedingly handsome moustache the ends of which he twisted a great deal with white, richly jewelled fingers. His air of dignity was heightened by three massive chins. He had a big trunk and an imposing corpulence so that when he sat at table he sat a little away from it, as though he ate under protest and were just there for a snack; but nature had played a dirty, though not uncommon trick on him; for his legs were much too short for his body so that, though seated he had all the appearance

of a tall man, you were taken aback to find when
he stood up that he was hardly of average height.
It was for this reason that he made his best effect
at table or when he was driving through the city
in his car. Then his presence was commanding.
When he waved to you or with a broad gesture
took off his hat, you felt that it was incredibly
affable of him to take any notice of human beings.
He had all the solid respectability of those states-
men of Louis Philippe, in sober black, with their
long hair and clean-shaven faces, who look out at
you with portentous solemnity from the canvases
of Ingres.

One often hears of people who talk like a book.
M. de Steenvoorde talked like a magazine, not of
course a magazine devoted to light literature and
the distraction of an idle hour, but a magazine
of sound learning and influential opinion. M. de
Steenvoorde talked like the *Revue des Deux
Mondes.* It was a treat, though a little fatiguing,
to listen to him. He had the fluency of those who
have said the same thing over and over again. He
never hesitated for a word. He put everything
with lucidity, an admirable choice of language, and
such an authority that in his lips the obvious had
all the sparkle of an epigram. He was by no
means without wit. He could be very amusing at
the expense of his neighbours. And when, having
said something peculiarly malicious, he turned to
you with an observation "*Les absents ont toujours
tort,*" he managed to invest it with the freshness
of an original aphorism. He was an ardent

Catholic, but, he flattered himself, no reactionary; a man of standing, substance, and principle.

A poor man, but ambitious (fame, the last infirmity of noble mind) he had married for her enormous dot the daughter of a sugar broker, now a painted little lady with hennaed hair, in beautiful clothes; and it must have been a sore trial to him that when he gave her his honoured name he could not also endow her with the sense of personal pride which was so powerful a motive in all his actions. For, like many great men, M. de Steenvoorde was married to a wife who was extremely unfaithful to him. But this misfortune he bore with a courage and a dignity which were absolutely characteristic. His demeanour was so perfect that his infelicity positively raised him in the eyes of his friends. He was to all an object of sympathy. He might be a cuckold, but he remained a person of quality. Whenever, indeed, Mme. de Steenvoorde took a new lover he insisted that her parents should give him a sufficient sum of money to make good the outrage to his name and honour. Common report put it at a quarter of a million francs, but with silver at its present price I believe that a business man would insist on being paid in dollars. M. de Steenvoorde is already a man of means, but before his wife reaches the canonical age he will undoubtedly be a rich one.

XX

THE BEAST OF BURDEN

AT first when you see the coolie on the
road, bearing his load, it is as a pleasing object that he strikes the eye. In
his blue rags, a blue of all colours from
indigo to turquoise and then to the paleness of a
milky sky, he fits the landscape. He seems exactly
right as he trudges along the narrow causeway
between the rice fields or climbs a green hill.
His clothing consists of no more than a short
coat and a pair of trousers; and if he had a
suit which was at the beginning all of a piece,
he never thinks when it comes to patching to
choose a bit of stuff of the same colour. He
takes anything that comes handy. From sun and
rain he protects his head with a straw hat shaped
like an extinguisher with a preposterously wide,
flat brim.

You see a string of coolies come along, one
after the other, each with a pole on his shoulders
from the ends of which hang two great bales, and
they make an agreeable pattern. It is amusing
to watch their hurrying reflections in the padi
water. You watch their faces as they pass you.
They are good-natured faces and frank, you would

have said, if it had not been drilled into you that the oriental is inscrutable; and when you see them lying down with their loads under a banyan tree by a wayside shrine, smoking and chatting gaily, if you have tried to lift the bales they carry for thirty miles or more a day, it seems natural to feel admiration for their endurance and their spirit. But you will be thought somewhat absurd if you mention your admiration to the old residents of China. You will be told with a tolerant shrug of the shoulders that the coolies are animals and for two thousand years from father to son have carried burdens, so it is no wonder if they do it cheerfully. And indeed you can see for yourself that they begin early, for you will encounter little children with a yoke on their shoulders staggering under the weight of vegetable baskets.

The day wears on and it grows warmer. The coolies take off their coats and walk stripped to the waist. Then sometimes in a man resting for an instant, his load on the ground but the pole still on his shoulders so that he has to rest slightly crouched, you see the poor tired heart beating against the ribs: you see it as plainly as in some cases of heart disease in the out-patients' room of a hospital. It is strangely distressing to watch. Then also you see the coolies' backs. The pressure of the pole for long years, day after day, has made hard red scars, and sometimes even there are open sores, great sores without bandages or dressing that rub against the wood; but the

78

strangest thing of all is that sometimes, as though
nature sought to adapt man for these cruel uses
to which he is put, an odd malformation seems
to have arisen so that there is a sort of hump, like
a camel's, against which the pole rests. But
beating heart or angry sore, bitter rain or burning sun notwithstanding, they go on eternally,
from dawn till dusk, year in year out, from childhood to the extreme of age. You see old men
without an ounce of fat on their bodies, their skin
loose on their bones, wizened, their little faces
wrinkled and apelike, with hair thin and grey; and
they totter under their burdens to the edge of
the grave in which at last they shall have rest
And still the coolies go, not exactly running, but
not walking either, sidling quickly, with their eyes
on the ground to choose the spot to place their
feet, and on their faces a strained, anxious expression. You can make no longer a pattern of them
as they wend their way. Their effort oppresses
you. You are filled with a useless compassion.

In China it is man that is the beast of burden.

*"To be harassed by the wear and tear of life,
and to pass rapidly through it without the possibility of arresting one's course,—is not this pitiful
indeed? To labour without ceasing, and then,
without living to enjoy the fruit, worn out, to
depart, suddenly, one knows not whither,—is not
that a just cause for grief?"*

So wrote the Chinese mystic.

XXI

DR. MACALISTER

HE was a fine figure of a man, hard upon sixty, I should think, when I knew him, but hale still and active. He was stout, but his great height enabled him to carry his corpulence with dignity. He had a strong, almost a handsome face, with a hooked nose, bushy white eyebrows and a firm chin. He was dressed in black, and he wore a low collar and a white bow tie. He had the look of an English divine of a past generation. His voice was resonant and hearty, and he laughed boisterously.

His career was somewhat out of the common. He had come to China thirty years before as a medical missionary, but now, though still on good terms with the mission, he was no longer a member. It had been decided, it appears, to build a school on a certain desirable spot which the doctor had hit upon, and in a crowded Chinese city it is never very easy to find building land, but when the mission after much bargaining had eventually bought this the discovery was made that the owner was not the Chinese with whom the negotiations had been conducted, but the doctor himself. Knowing that the school must be built and seeing that no other piece of land was available he had borrowed money from a Chinese banker and bought it himself. The transaction was not dishonest, but perhaps it was a little unscrupulous and the other members of the mission did not look upon it as the good joke that Dr. Macalister did. They displayed even a certain acrimony, and the result was that Dr. Macalister, though preserving friendly relations with persons with whose aims and interests he was in the fullest sympathy, resigned his position. He was known to be a clever doctor and he soon had a large practice both among the foreigners and the Chinese. He started a hostel in which the traveller, at a price, and a high one, could have board and lodging. His guests complained a little because they were not allowed to drink alcohol, but it was much more comfortable than a Chinese inn, and some allowance had to be made for the doctor's principles. He was a man of resource. He bought a large piece of land on a hill on the other side of the river and put up bungalows which he sold one by one to the missionaries as summer resorts; and he owned a large store in which he sold everything, from picture postcards and curios to Worcester sauce and knitted jumpers, which a foreigner could possibly want. He made a very good thing out of it. He had a commercial bent.

The tiffin he invited me to was quite an imposing function. He lived above his store in a large apartment overlooking the river. The party consisted of Dr. Macalister and his third wife, a lady of forty-five in gold-rimmed spectacles and black satin, a missionary spending a few days with the doctor on his way into the interior, and two silent young ladies who had just joined the mission and were busily learning Chinese. On the walls of the dining-room hung a number of congratulatory scrolls which had been presented to my host by Chinese friends and converts on his fiftieth birthday. There was a great deal of food, as there always is in China, and Dr. Macalister did full justice to it. The meal began and ended with a long grace which he said in his deep voice, with an impressive unction.

When we returned to the drawing-room Dr. Macalister, standing in front of the grateful fire, for it can be very cold in China, took a little photograph from the chimney piece and showed it to me.

"Do you know who that is?" he asked.

It was the photograph of a very thin young missionary in a low collar and a white tie, with large melancholy eyes and a look of profound seriousness.

"Nice looking fellow, eh?" boomed the doctor.

"Very," I answered.

A somewhat priggish young man possibly, but priggishness is a pardonable defect in youth, and here it was certainly counterbalanced by the appealing wistfulness of the expression. It was a fine, a sensitive, and even a beautiful face, and those disconsolate eyes were strangely moving. There was fanaticism there, perhaps, but there was the courage that would not fear martyrdom; there was a charming idealism; and its youth, its ingenuousness, warmed one's heart.

"A most attractive face," I said as I returned the photograph.

Dr. Macalister gave a chuckle.

"That's what I looked like when I first came out to China," he said.

It was a photograph of himself.

"No one recognises it," smiled Mrs. Macalister.

"It was the very image of me," he said.

He spread out the tails of his black coat and planted himself more firmly in front of the fire.

"I often laugh when I think of my first impressions of China," he said. "I came out expecting to undergo hardships and privations. My first shock was the steamer with ten-course dinners and first-class accommodation. There wasn't much hardship in that, but I said to myself: wait till you get to China. Well, at Shanghai I was met by some friends and I stayed in a fine house and was waited on by fine servants and I ate fine food. Shanghai, I said, the plague spot of the East. It'll be different in the interior. At last I reached here. I was to stay with the head of the mission till my own quarters were ready. He lived in a large compound. He had a very nice house with American furniture in it and I slept in a better bed than I'd ever slept in. He was very fond of his garden and he grew all kinds of vegetables in it. We had salads just like the salads we had in America and fruit, all kinds of fruit;

he kept a cow and we had fresh milk and butter.
I thought I'd never eaten so much and so well in
my life. You did nothing for yourself. If you
wanted a glass of water you called a boy and he
brought it to you. It was the beginning of summer when I arrived and they were all packing up
to go to the hills. They hadn't got bungalows
then, but they used to spend the summer in a
temple. I began to think I shouldn't have to put
up with much privation after all. I had been
looking forward to a martyr's crown. Do you
know what I did?"

Dr. Macalister chuckled as he thought of that
long passed time.

"The first night I got here, when I was alone
in my room, I threw myself on my bed and I just
cried like a child."

Dr. Macalister went on talking, but I could not
pay much attention to what he said. I wondered
by what steps he had come to be the man I knew
now from the man he had been then. That is the
story I should like to write.

XXII

THE ROAD

IT is not a road at all but a causeway, made
of paving stones about a foot wide and four
feet broad so that there is just room for
two sedan chairs with caution to pass each
other. For the most part it is in good enough
repair, but here and there the stones are broken
or swept away by the flooding of the rice fields,
and then walking is difficult. It winds tortuously
along the path which has connected city to city
since first a thousand years ago or more there
were cities in the land. It winds between the rice
fields following the accidents of the country with a
careful nonchalance; and you can tell that it was
built on a track made by the peasant of dim ages
past who sought not the quickest but the easiest
way to walk. The beginnings of it you may see
when, leaving the main road you cut across country, bound for some town that is apart from the
main line of traffic. Then the causeway is so narrow that there is no room for a coolie bearing a
load to pass and if you are in the midst of the
rice fields he has to get on the little bank, planted
with beans, that divides one from another, till you
go by. Presently the stones are wanting and you

travel along a path of trodden mud so narrow
that your bearers step warily.

The journey, for all the stories of bandits with
which they sought to deter you, and the ragged
soldiers of your escort, is devoid of adventure;
but it is crowded with incident. First there is
the constant variety of the dawn. Poets have
written of it with enthusiasm, but they are lie-a-
beds, and they have trusted for inspiration to
their fancy rather than to their sleepy eyes. Like
a mistress known in the dream of a moonlit night
who has charms unshared by the beauties of the
wakeful day, they have ascribed to it excellencies
which are only of the imagination. For the most
exquisite dawn has none of the splendour of an
indifferent sunset. But because it is a less accustomed sight it seems to have a greater diversity.
Every dawn is a little different from every other,
and you can fancy that each day the world is
created anew not quite the same as it was the day
before.

Then there are the common sights of the way-
side. A peasant, thigh deep in water, ploughs his
field with a plough as primitive as those his fathers
have used for forty mortal centuries. The water
buffalo splashes sinister through the mud and his
cynical eyes seem to ask what end has been served
by this unending toil. An old woman goes by in
her blue smock and short blue trousers, on bound
feet, and she supports her unsteady steps with a
long staff. Two fat Chinese in chairs pass you,
and passing stare at you with curious yet listless

eyes. Everyone you see is an incident, however trivial, sufficient to arouse your fancy for an instant; and now your eyes rest with pleasure on the smooth skin, like yellow ivory, of a young mother sauntering along with a child strapped to her back, on the wrinkled, inscrutable visage of an old man, or on the fine bones, visible through the flesh of the face, of a strapping coolie. And beside all this there is the constant delight with which, having climbed laboriously a hill, you see the country spread out before you. For days and days it just the same, but each time you see it you have the same little thrill of discovery. The same little rounded hills, like a flock of sheep, surrounding you, succeeding one another as far as the eye can reach; and on many, a lone tree, as though planted deliberately for the sake of the picturesque, outlines its gracious pattern against the sky. The same groves of bamboo lean delicately, almost surrounding the same farm houses, which with their clustering roofs nestle pleasantly in the same sheltered hollows. The bamboos lean over the highway with an adorable grace. They have the condescension of great ladies which flatters rather than wounds. They have the abandon of flowers, a well-born wantonness that is too sure of its good breeding ever to be in danger of debauchery. But the memorial arch, to virtuous widow or to fortunate scholar, warns you that you are approaching a village or a town, and you pass, affording a moment's sensation to the inhabitants, through a ragged line of sordid hovels or a busy street. The street is shaded from the sun by great mats stretched from eave to eave; the light is dim and the thronging crowd has an unnatural air. You think that so must have looked the people in those cities of magicians which the Arab traveller knew, and where during the night a terrible transformation befell you so that till you found the magic formula to free you, you went through life in the guise of a one-eyed ass or of a green and yellow parrot. The merchants in their open shops seem to sell no common merchandise and in the taverns messes are prepared of things horrible for men to eat. Your eye, amid the uniformity, for every Chinese town, at all events to the stranger's eye, much resembles every other, takes pleasure in noting trivial differences, and so you observe the predominant industries of each one. Every town makes all that its inhabitants require, but it has also a speciality, and here you will find cotton cloth, there string, and here again silk. Now the orange tree, golden with fruit, grows scarce and the sugar cane makes its appearance. The black silk cap gives way to the turban and the red umbrella of oiled paper to the umbrella of bright blue cotton.

But these are the common incidents of every day. They are like the expected happenings of life which keep it from monotony, working days and holidays, meetings with your friends, the coming of spring with its elation and the coming of winter with its long evenings, its easy intimacies and its twilight. Now and then, as love enters making all the rest but a setting for its radiance and lifts the common affairs of the day to a level on which the most trifling things have a mysterious significance, now and then the common round is interrupted and you are faced by a beauty which takes your soul, all unprepared, by assault. For looming through the mist you may see the fantastic roofs of a temple loftily raised on a huge stone bastion, around which, a natural moat, flows a quiet green river, and when the sun lights it you seem to see the dream of a Chinese palace, a palace as rich and splendid as those which haunted the fancy of the Arabian story tellers; or, crossing a ferry at dawn you may see, a little above you, silhouetted against the sunrise, a sampan in which a ferryman is carrying a crowd of passengers; you recognise on a sudden Charon, and you know that his passengers are the melancholy dead.

XXIII

GOD'S TRUTH

BIRCH was the agent of the B. A. T. and he was stationed in a little town of the interior with streets which, after it had rained, were a foot deep in mud. Then you had to get right inside your cart to prevent yourself from being splashed from head to foot. The roadway, worn to pieces by the ceaseless traffic, was so full of holes that the breath was jolted out of your body as you jogged along at a foot pace. There were two or three streets of shops, but he knew by heart everything that was in them; and there were interminable winding alleys which presented a monotonous expanse of wall broken only by solid closed doors. These were the Chinese houses and they were as impenetrable to one of his colour as the life which surrounded him. He was very homesick. He had not spoken to a white man for three months.

His day's work was over. Since he had nothing else to do he went for the only walk there was. He went out of the city gate and strolled along the ragged road, with its deep ruts, into the country. The valley was bounded by wild, barren mountains and they seemed to shut him in. He felt immeasurably far away from civilisation. He knew he could not afford to surrender to that sense of utter loneliness which beset him, but it was more of an effort than usual to keep a stiff upper lip. He was very nearly at the end of his tether. Suddenly he saw a white man riding towards him on a pony. Behind came slowly a Chinese cart in which presumably were his belongings. Birch guessed at once that this was a missionary going down to one of the treaty-ports from his station further up country, and his heart leaped with joy. At last he would have some one to talk to. He hurried his steps. His lassitude left him. He was all alert. He was almost running when he came up to the rider.

"Hulloa," he said, "where have you sprung from?"

The rider stopped and named a distant town.

"I am on my way down to take the train," he added.

"You'd better put up with me for the night. I haven't seen a white man for three months. There's lots of room at my place. B. A. T. you know."

"B. A. T.," said the rider. His face changed and his eyes, before friendly and smiling, grew hard. "I don't want to have anything to do with you."

He gave his pony a kick and started on, but Birch seized the bridle. He could not believe his ears.

"What do you mean?"

"I can't have anything to do with a man who trades in tobacco. Let go that bridle."

"But I've not spoken to a white man for three months."

"That's no business of mine. Let go that bridle."

He gave his pony another kick. His lips were obstinately set and he looked at Birch sternly. Then Birch lost his temper. He clung to the bridle as the pony moved on and began to curse the missionary. He hurled at him every term of abuse he could think of. He swore. He was horribly obscene. The missionary did not answer, but urged his pony on. Birch seized the missionary's leg and jerked it out of the stirrup; the missionary nearly fell off and he clung in a somewhat undignified fashion to the pony's mane. Then he half slipped, half tumbled to the ground. The cart had come up to them by now and stopped. The two Chinese who were sitting in it looked at the white men with indolent curiosity. The missionary was livid with rage.

"You've assaulted me. I'll have you fired for that."

"You can go to hell," said Birch. "I haven't seen a white man for three months and you won't even speak to me. Do you call yourself a Christian?"

"What is your name?"

"Birch is my name and be damned to you."

"I shall report you to your chief. Now stand back and let me get on my journey."

Birch clenched his hands.

"Get a move on or I'll break every bone in your body."

The missionary mounted, gave his pony a sharp cut with the whip, and cantered away. The Chinese cart lumbered slowly after. But when Birch was left alone his anger left him and a sob broke unwillingly from his lips. The barren mountains were less hard than the heart of man. He turned and walked slowly back to the little walled city.

XXIV

ROMANCE

ALL day I had been dropping down the river. This was the river up which Chang Chien, seeking its source, had sailed for many days till he came to a city where he saw a girl spinning and a youth leading an ox to the water. He asked what place this was and in reply the girl gave him her shuttle telling him to show it on his return to the astrologer Yen Chün-ping, who would thus know where he had been. He did so and the astrologer at once recognised the shuttle as that of the Spinning Damsel, further declaring that on the day and at the hour when Chang Chien received the shuttle he had noticed a wandering star intrude itself between the Spinning Damsel and the Cowherd. So Chang Chien knew that he had sailed upon the bosom of the Milky Way.

I, however, had not been so far. All day, as for seven days before, my five rowers, standing up, had rowed, and there rang still in my ears the monotonous sound of their oars against the wooden pin that served as rowlock. Now and again the water became very shallow and there was a jar and a jolt as we scraped along the stones of the river bed. Then two or three of the rowers turned up their blue trousers to the hip and let themselves over the side. Shouting they dragged the flat-bottomed boat over the shoal. Now and again we came to a rapid, of no great consequence when compared with the turbulent rapids of the Yangtze, but sufficiently swift to call for trackers to pull the junks that were going up stream; and we, going down, passed through them with many shouts, shot the foaming breakers and presently reached water as smooth as any lake.

Now it was night and my crew were asleep, forward, huddled together in such shelter as they had been able to rig up when we moored at dusk. I sat on my bed. Bamboo matting spread over three wooden arches made the sorry cabin which for a week had served me as parlour and bedroom. It was closed at one end by matchboarding so roughly put together that there were large chinks between each board. The bitter wind blew through them. It was on the other side of this that the crew—fine sturdy fellows—rowed by day and slept by night, joined then by the steersman who had stood from dawn to dusk, in a tattered blue gown and a wadded coat of faded grey, a black turban round his head, at the long oar which was his helm. There was no furniture but my bed, a shallow dish like an enormous soup-plate in which burned charcoal, for it was cold, a basket containing my clothes which I used as a table, and a hurricane lamp which hung from one of the arches and swayed slightly with the motion of the water.

The cabin was so low that I, a person of no great height (I comfort myself with Bacon's observation that with tall men it is as with tall houses, the top story is commonly the least furnished) could only just stand upright. One of the sleepers began to snore more loudly, and perhaps he awoke two of the others, for I heard the sound of speaking; but presently this ceased, the snorer was quiet, and all about me once more was silence.

Then suddenly I had a feeling that here, facing me, touching me almost, was the romance I sought. It was a feeling like no other, just as specific as the thrill of art; but I could not for the life of me tell what it was that had given me just then that rare emotion.

In the course of my life I have been often in situations which, had I read of them, would have seemed to me sufficiently romantic; but it is only in retrospect, comparing them with my ideas of what was romantic, that I have seen them as at all out of the ordinary. It is only by an effort of the imagination, making myself as it were a spectator of myself acting a part, that I have caught anything of the precious quality in circumstances which in others would have seemed to me instinct with its fine flower. When I have danced with an actress whose fascination and whose genius made her the idol of my country, or wandered through the halls of some great house in which was gathered all that was distinguished by lineage or intellect that London could show, I have only recognized afterwards that here perhaps, though in somewhat Ouidaesque a fashion, was romance. In battle, when, myself in no great danger, I was able to watch events with a thrill of interest, I had not the phlegm to assume the part of a spectator. I have sailed through the night, under the full moon, to a coral island in the Pacific, and then the beauty and the wonder of the scene gave me a conscious happiness, but only later the exhilarating sense that romance and I had touched fingers. I heard the flutter of its wings when once, in the bedroom of a hotel in New York, I sat round a table with half a dozen others and made plans to restore an ancient kingdom whose wrongs have for a century inspired the poet and the patriot; but my chief feeling was a surprised amusement that through the hazards of war I found myself engaged in business so foreign to my bent. The authentic thrill of romance has seized me under circumstances which one would have thought far less romantic, and I remember that I knew it first one evening when I was playing cards in a cottage on the coast of Brittany. In the next room an old fisherman lay dying and the women of the house said that he would go out with the tide. Without a storm was raging and it seemed fit for the last moments of that aged warrior of the seas that his going should be accompanied by the wild cries of the wind as it hurled itself against the shuttered windows. The waves thundered upon the tortured rocks. I felt a sudden exultation, for I knew that here was romance.

And now the same exultation seized me, and once more romance, like a bodily presence, was before me. But it had come so unexpectedly that I was intrigued. I could not tell whether it had crept in among the shadows that the lamp threw on the bamboo matting or whether it was wafted down the river that I saw through the opening of my cabin. Curious to know what were the elements that made up the ineffable delight of the moment I went out to the stern of the boat. Alongside were moored half a dozen junks, going up river, for their masts were erect; and everything was silent in them. Their crews were long since asleep. The night was not dark, for though it was cloudy the moon was full, but the river in that veiled light was ghostly. A vague mist blurred the trees on the further bank. It was an enchanting sight, but there was in it nothing unaccustomed and what I sought was not there. I turned away. But when I returned to my bamboo shelter the magic which had given it so extraordinary a character was gone. Alas, I was like a man who should tear a butterfly to pieces in order to discover in what its beauty lay. And yet, as Moses descending from Mount Sinai wore on his face a brightness from his converse with the God of Israel, my little cabin, my dish of charcoal, my lamp, even my camp bed, had still about them something of the thrill which for a moment was mine. I could not see them any more quite indifferently, because for a moment I had seen them magically.

XXV

THE GRAND STYLE

HE was a very old man. It was fifty-seven years since he came to China as a ship's doctor and took the place in one of the Southern ports of a medical officer whose health had obliged him to go home. He could not then have been less than twenty-five so that now he must have been well over eighty. He was a tall man, very thin, and his skin hung on his bones like a suit of clothes much too large for him: under his chin was a great sack like the wattle of an old turkey-cock; but his blue eyes, large and bright, had kept their colour, and his voice was strong and deep. In these seven and fifty years he had bought and sold three or four practices along the coast and now he was back once more within a few miles of the port in which he had first lived. It was an anchorage at the mouth of the river where the steamers, unable owing to their draught to reach the city, dis-charged and loaded their cargo. There were only seven white men's houses, a small hospital, and a handful of Chinese, so that it would not have been worth a doctor's while to settle there; but he was vice-consul as well, and the easy life at his great age just suited him. There was enough to do to prevent him from feeling idle, but not enough to tire him. His spirit was still hale.

"I'm thinking of retiring," he said, "it's about time I gave the youngsters a chance."

He amused himself with plans for the future: all his life he had wanted to visit the West Indies and upon his soul he meant to now. By George, Sir, he couldn't afford to leave it much longer. England? Well, from all he heard England was no place for a gentleman nowadays. He was last there thirty years ago. Besides he wasn't English. He was born in Ireland. Yes, Sir, he took his degree at Trinity College, Dublin; but what with the priests on one side and the Sinn Feiners on the other he could not believe there was much left of the Ireland he knew as a boy. A fine country to hunt in, he said, with a gleam in his open blue eyes.

He had better manners than are usually found in the medical profession which, though blest with many virtues, neglects somewhat the amenities of polite behaviour. I do not know whether it is commerce with the sick which gives the doctor an unfortunate sense of superiority; the example of his teachers some of whom have still a bad tradition of rudeness which certain eminent practitioners of the past cultivated as a professional asset; or his early training among the poor patients of a hospital whom he is apt to look upon as of a lower class than himself; but it is certain

100

that no body of men is on the whole so wanting
in civility.

He was very different from the men of my generation; but whether the difference lay in his voice
and gesture, in the ease of his manner, or in the
elaborateness of his antique courtesy, it was not
easy to discover. I think he was more definitely
a gentleman than people are nowadays when a
man is a gentleman with deprecation. The word
is in bad odour and the qualities it denotes have
come in for a deal of ridicule. Persons who by
no stretch of the fancy could be so described have
made a great stir in the world during the last
thirty years and they have used all the resources
of their sarcasm to render odious a title which
they are perhaps all too conscious of never de-
serving. Perhaps also the difference in him was
due to a difference of education. In his youth he
had been taught much useless learning, the classics
of Greece and Rome, and they had given a foundation to his character which in the present is somewhat rare. He was young in an age which did
not know the weekly press and when the monthly
magazine was a staid affair. Reading was more
solid. Perhaps men drank more than was good
for them, but they read Horace for pleasure and
they knew by heart the novels of Sir Walter Scott.
He remembered reading *The Newcomes* when it
came out. I think the men of that time were, if
not more adventurous than the men of ours, more
adventurous in the grand manner: now a man will

risk his life with a joke from *Comic Cuts* on his lips, then it was with a Latin quotation.

But how can I analyse the subtle quality which distinguished this old man? Read a page of Swift: the words are the same as those we use to-day and there is hardly a sentence in which they are not placed in the simplest order; and yet there is a dignity, a spaciousness, an aroma, which all our modern effort fails to attain: in short there is style. And so with him; there was style, and there is no more to be said.

XXVI

RAIN

YES, but the sun does not shine every day. Sometimes a cold rain beats down on you and a northeast wind chills you to the bone. Your shoes and your coat are wet still from the day before and you have three hours to go before breakfast. You tramp along in the cheerless light of that bitter dawn, with thirty miles before you and nothing to look forward to at the end but the squalid discomfort of a Chinese inn. There you will find bare walls, a clammy floor of trodden earth, and you will dry yourself as best you can over a dish of burning charcoal.

Then you think of your pleasant room in London. The rain driving in squalls against the windows only makes its warmth more grateful. You sit by the fire, your pipe in your mouth, and read the *Times* from cover to cover, not the leading articles of course but the agony column and the advertisements of country houses you will never be able to afford. (On the Chiltern Hills, standing in its own park of one hundred and fifty acres, with spacious garden, orchard, etc., a Georgian house in perfect condition, with original woodwork and chimney pieces, six reception rooms, fourteen bedrooms and usual offices, modern sanitation, stabling with rooms over and excellent garage. Three miles from first rate golf course.) I know then that Messrs. Knight, Frank, and Rutley are my favourite authors. The matters that they treat of like the great commonplaces which are the material of all fine poetry never stale; and their manner like that of the best masters is characteristic but at the same time various. Their style, as is that of Confucius according to the sinologues, is glitteringly compact: succinct but suggestive it combines an admirable exactness with a breadth of image which gives the imagination an agreeable freedom. Their mastery of words such as rood and perch of which I suppose I once knew the meaning but which for many years have been a mystery to me, is amazing, and they will use them with ease and assurance. They can play with technical terms with the ingenuity of Mr. Rudyard Kipling and they can invest them with the Celtic glamour of Mr. W. B. Yeats. They have combined their individualities so completely that I defy the most discerning critic to discover traces of a divided authorship. Literary history is acquainted with the collaboration of two writers, and the names of Beaumont and Fletcher, Erckman Chatrian, Besant and Rice spring to the excited fancy; but now that the higher criticism has destroyed that belief in the triple authorship of the Bible which I was taught in my youth, I conjecture that the case of Knight, Frank and Rutley is unique.

Then Elizabeth, very smart in the white squirrel I brought her from China, comes in to say good-bye to me, for she, poor child, must go out whatever the weather, and I play trains with her while her pram is being got ready. Then of course I should do a little work, but the weather is so bad that I feel lazy, and I take up instead Professor Giles' book on Chuang-Tzu. The rigid Confucianists frown upon him because he is an individualist, and it is to the individualism of the age that they ascribe the lamentable decay of China, but he is very good reading; he has the advantage on a rainy day that he can be read without great application and not seldom you come across a thought that sets your own wandering. But presently ideas, insinuating themselves into your consciousness like the lapping waves of a rising tide, absorb you to the exclusion of those which old Chuang-Tzu suggested, and notwithstanding your desire to idle, you sit down at your table. Only the dilettante uses a desk. Your pen goes easily and you write without effort. It is very good to be alive. Then two amusing people come to luncheon and when they are gone you drop into Christie's. You see some Ming figures there, but they are not so good as those you brought from China yourself, and then you watch being sold pictures you are only too glad not to possess. You look at your watch; there is pretty sure to be a rubber

going at the Garrick, and the shocking weather
justifies you in wasting the rest of the afternoon.
You cannot stay very late, for you have seats for
a first night and you must get home and dress
for an early dinner. You will be just in time
to tell Elizabeth a little story before she goes to
sleep. She looks really very nice in her pyjamas
with her hair done up in two plaits. There is
something about a first night which only the
satiety of the critic can fail to be moved by. It
is pleasant to see your friends and amusing to
hear the pit's applause when a favourite of the
stage, acting, better than she ever does behind the
footlights, a delightful embarrassment at being
recognised, advances to take her seat. It may
be a bad play that you are going to see, but it has
at least the merit that no one has seen it before;
and there is always the chance of a moment's
emotion or of a smile.

Towards you in their great straw hats, like the
hat of love-sick Pierrot, but with a huge brim,
come a string of coolies, lolloping along, bent forward a little under the weight of the great bales
of cotton that they carry. The rain plasters
their blue clothes, so thin and ragged, against
their bodies. The broken stones of the causeway
are slippery, and with toil you pick your muddy
way.

XXVII

SULLIVAN

HE was an Irish sailor. He deserted his ship at Hong-Kong and took it into his head to walk across China. He spent three years wandering about the country, and soon acquired a very good knowledge of Chinese. He learned it, as is common among men of his class, with greater ease than do the more highly educated. He lived on his wits. He made a point of avoiding the British Consul, but went to the magistrate of each town he came to and represented himself as having been robbed on the way of all his money. His story was not improbable and it was told with a wealth of convincing detail which would have excited the admiration of so great a master as Captain Costigan. The magistrate, after the Chinese fashion, was anxious to get rid of him and was glad to do so at the cost of ten or fifteen dollars. If he could get no money he could generally count on a place to sleep in and a good meal. He had a certain rough humour which appealed to the Chinese. So he continued very successfully till he hit by misfortune on a magistrate of a different stamp. This man when he told his story said to him:

"You are nothing but a beggar and a vagabond. You must be beaten."

He gave an order and the fellow was promptly taken out, thrown on the ground, and soundly thrashed. He was not only very much hurt, but exceedingly surprised, and what is more strangely mortified. It ruined his nerve. There and then he gave up his vagrant life and making his way to one of the out-ports applied to the commissioner of customs for a place as tide-waiter. It is not easy to find white men to take such posts and few questions are asked of those who seek them. He was given a job and you may see him now, a sun-burned, clean-shaven man of forty-five, florid and rather stout, in a neat blue uniform, boarding the steamers and the junks at a little riverside town, where the deputy-commissioner, the postmaster, a missionary, and he are the only Europeans. His knowledge of the Chinese and their ways makes him an invaluable servant. He has a little yellow wife and four children. He has no shame about his past and over a good stiff whisky he will tell you the whole story of his adventurous travels. But the beating is what he can never get over. It surprises him yet and he cannot, he simply cannot understand it. He has no ill-feeling towards the magistrate who ordered it; on the contrary it appeals to his sense of humour.

"He was a great old sportsman, the old blackguard," he says. "Nerve, eh?"

XXVIII

THE DINING-ROOM

IT was an immense room in an immense house. When it was built, building was cheap, and the merchant princes of that day built magnificently. Money was made easily then and life was luxurious. It was not hard to make a fortune and a man, almost before he had reached middle age, could return to England and live the rest of his days no less splendidly in a fine house in Surrey. It is true that the population was hostile and it was always possible that a riot might make it necessary for him to fly for his life, but this only added a spice to the comfort of his existence; and when danger threatened it was fairly certain that a gunboat would arrive in time to offer protection or refuge. The foreign community, largely allied by marriage, was sociable, and its members entertained one another lavishly. They gave pompous dinner parties, they danced together, and they played whist. Work was not so pressing that it was impossible to spend now and again a few days in the interior shooting duck. It was certainly very hot in summer, and after a few years a man was apt to take things easily, but the rest of the year was only warm, with blue skies and a balmy air, and life was very pleasant. There was a certain liberty of behaviour and no one was thought the worse of, so long as the matter was not intruded on the notice of the ladies, if he had to live with him a little bright-eyed Chinese girl. When he married he sent her away with a present and if there were children they were provided for at a Eurasian school in Shanghai.

But this agreeable life was a thing of the past. The port lived on its export of tea and the change of taste from Chinese to Ceylon had ruined it. For thirty years the port had lain a-dying. Before that the consul had had two vice-consuls to help him in his work, but now he was able to do it easily by himself. He generally managed to get a game of golf in the afternoon and he was seldom too busy for a rubber of bridge. Nothing remained of the old splendour but the enormous hongs, and they were mostly empty. The tea merchants, such as were left of them, turned their hands to all manner of side lines in the effort to make both ends meet. But the effort was listless. Everyone in the port seemed old. It was no place for a young man.

And in the room in which I sat I seemed to read the history of the past and the history of the man I was awaiting. It was Sunday morning and when I arrived after two days on a coasting steamer, he was in church. I tried to construct a portrait of him from the room. There was something pathetic about it. It had the magnificence of a past generation, but a magnificence run to seed, and its tidiness, I know not why, seemed to emphasize a shame-faced poverty. On the floor was a huge Turkey carpet which in the seventies must have cost a great deal of money, but now it was quite threadbare. The immense mahogany table, at which so many good dinners had been eaten, with such a luxury of wine, was so highly polished that you could see your face in it. It suggested port, old and tawny, and prosperous, red faced gentlemen with side whiskers discussing the antics of the mountebank Disraeli. The walls were of that sombre red which was thought suitable for a dining room when dinner was a respectable function and they were heavy with pictures. Here were the father and mother of my host, an elderly gentleman with grey whiskers and a bald head and a stern dark old lady with her hair dressed in the fashion of the Empress Eugenie, and there his grandfather in a stock and his grandmother in a mob cap. The mahogany sideboard with a mirror at the back, was laden with plated salvers, and a tea service, and much else, while in the middle of the dining table stood an immense épergne. On the black marble chimney piece was a black marble clock, flanked by black marble vases, and in the four corners of the room were cabinets filled with all manner of plated articles. Here and there great palms in pots spread their stiff foliage. The chairs were of massive mahogany, stuffed, and covered with faded red leather, and on each side of the fireplace was an arm-chair. The room, large though it was, seemed crowded, but because

111

everything was rather shabby it gave you an impression of melancholy. All those things seemed to have a sad life of their own, but a life subdued, as though the force of circumstances had proved too much for them. They had no longer the strength to struggle against fate, but they clung together with a tremulous eagerness as though they had a vague feeling that only so could they retain their significance, and I felt that it was only a little time before the end came when they would lie haphazard, in an unlovely confusion, with little numbers pasted on them, in the dreary coldness of an auction room.

XXIX

ARABESQUE

THERE in the mist, enormous, majestic, silent, and terrible, stood the Great Wall of China. Solitarily, with the indifference of nature herself, it crept up the mountain side and slipped down to the depth of the valley. Menacingly, the grim watch towers, stark and foursquare, at due intervals stood at their posts. Ruthlessly, for it was built at the cost of a million lives and each one of those great grey stones has been stained with the bloody tears of the captive and the outcast, it forged its dark way through a sea of rugged mountains. Fearlessly, it went on its endless journey, league upon league to the furthermost regions of Asia, in utter solitude, mysterious like the great empire it guarded. There in the mist, enormous, majestic, silent, and terrible, stood the Great Wall of China.

XXX

THE CONSUL

MR. PETE was in a state of the liveliest exasperation. He had been in the consular service for more than twenty years and he had had to deal with all manner of vexatious people, officials who would not listen to reason, merchants who took the British Government for a debt collecting agency, missionaries who resented as gross injustice any attempt at fair play; but he never recollected a case which had left him more completely at a loss. He was a mild-mannered man, but for no reason he flew into a passion with his writer and he very nearly sacked the Eurasian clerk because he had wrongly spelt two words in a letter placed before him for his official signature. He was a conscientious man and he could not persuade himself to leave his office before the clock struck four, but the moment it did he jumped up and called for his hat and stick. Because his boy did not bring them at once he abused him roundly. They say that the consuls all grow a little odd; and the merchants who can live for thirty-five years in China without learning enough of the language to ask their way in the street, say that it is because they

have to study Chinese; and there was no doubt
that Mr. Pete was decidedly odd. He was a
bachelor and on that account had been sent to a
series of posts which by reason of their isolation
were thought unsuited to married men. He had
lived so much alone that his natural tendency to
eccentricity had developed to an extravagant degree, and he had habits which surprised the
stranger. He was very absent-minded. He
paid no attention to his house, which was always
in great disorder, nor to his food; his boys gave
him to eat what they liked and for everything he
had made him pay through the nose. He was un-
tiring in his efforts to suppress the opium traffic,
but he was the only person in the city who did not
know that his servants kept opium in the consulate
itself, and a busy traffic in the drug was openly
conducted at the back door of the compound. He
was an ardent collector and the house provided
for him by the government was filled with the
various things which he had collected one after
the other, pewter, brass, carved wood; these were
his more legitimate enterprises; but he also collected stamps, birds' eggs, hotel labels, and postmarks: he boasted that he had a collection of
postmarks which was unequalled in the Empire.
During his long sojourning in lonely places he
had read a great deal, and though he was no
sinologue he had a greater knowledge of China,
its history, literature, and people, than most of
his colleagues; but from his wide reading he had
acquired not toleration but vanity. He was a

man of a singular appearance. His body was small and frail and when he walked he gave you the idea of a dead leaf dancing before the wind; and then there was something extraordinarily odd in the small Tyrolese hat, with a cock's feather in it, very old and shabby, which he wore perched rakishly on the side of his large head. He was exceedingly bald. You saw that his eyes, blue and pale, were weak behind the spectacles, and a drooping, ragged, dingy moustache did not hide the peevishness of his mouth. And now, turning out of the street in which was the consulate, he made his way on to the city wall, for there only in the multitudinous city was it possible to walk with comfort.

He was a man who took his work hardly, worrying himself to death over every trifle, but as a rule a walk on the wall soothed and rested him. The city stood in the midst of a great plain and often at sundown from the wall you could see in the distance the snow-capped mountains, the mountains of Tibet; but now he walked quickly, looking neither to the right nor to the left, and his fat spaniel frisked about him unobserved. He talked to himself rapidly in a low monotone. The cause of his irritation was a visit that he had that day received from a lady who called herself Mrs. Yü and whom he with a consular passion for precision insisted on calling Miss Lambert. This in itself sufficed to deprive their intercourse of amenity. She was an Englishwoman married to a Chinese. She had arrived two years before with

116

her husband from England where he had been
studying at the University of London; he had
made her believe that he was a great personage
in his own country and she had imagined herself
to be coming to a gorgeous palace and a position
of consequence. It was a bitter surprise when
she found herself brought to a shabby Chinese
house crowded with people: there was not even a
foreign bed in it, nor a knife and fork:
everything seemed to her very dirty and smelly.
It was a shock to find that she had to live with
her husband's father and mother and he told her
that she must do exactly what his mother bade
her; but in her complete ignorance of Chinese it
was not till she had been two or three days in the
house that she realised that she was not her husband's only wife. He had been married as a boy
before he left his native city to acquire the knowledge of the barbarians. When she bitterly upbraided him for deceiving her he shrugged his
shoulders. There was nothing to prevent a Chinese from having two wives if he wanted them and,
he added with some disregard to truth, no Chinese
woman looked upon it as a hardship. It was
upon making this discovery that she paid her first
visit to the consul. He had already heard of her
arrival—in China everyone knows everything
about everyone—and he received her without surprise. Nor had he much sympathy to show her.
That a foreign woman should marry a Chinese at
all filled him with indignation, but that she should
do so without making proper inquiries vexed him

like a personal affront. She was not at all the sort
of woman whose appearance led you to imagine
that she would be guilty of such a folly. She was
a solid, thick-set, young person, short, plain, and
matter of fact. She was cheaply dressed in a
tailor-made suit and she wore a Tam-o'-shanter.
She had bad teeth and a muddy skin. Her hands
were large and red and ill cared for. You could
tell that she was not unused to hard work. She
spoke English with a Cockney whine.

"How did you meet Mr. Yü?" asked the consul
frigidly.

"Well, you see, it's like this," she answered.
"Dad was in a very good position, and when he
died mother said: 'Well, it seems a sinful waste
to keep all these rooms empty, I'll put a card in
the window.' "

The consul interrupted her.

"He had lodgings with you?"

"Well, they weren't exactly lodgings," she said.

"Shall we say apartments then?" replied the
consul, with his thin, slightly vain smile.

That was generally the explanation of these
marriages. Then because he thought her a very
foolish vulgar woman he explained bluntly that
according to English law she was not married to
Yü and that the best thing she could do was to
go back to England at once. She began to cry
and his heart softened a little to her. He prom-
ised to put her in charge of some missionary ladies
who would look after her on the long journey, and
indeed, if she liked, he would see if meanwhile she

118

could not live in one of the missions. But while
he talked Miss Lambert dried her tears.

"What's the good of going back to England?"
she said at last. "I 'aven't got nowhere to go to "

"You can go to your mother."

"She was all against my marrying Mr. Yü. I
should never hear the last of it if I was to go back
now."

The consul began to argue with her, but the
more he argued the more determined she became,
and at last he lost his temper.

"If you like to stay here with a man who isn't
your husband it's your own look out, but I wash
my hands of all responsibility."

Her retort had often rankled.

"Then you've got no cause to worry," she said,
and the look on her face returned to him whenever he thought of her.

That was two years ago and he had seen her
once or twice since then. It appeared that she
got on very badly both with her mother-in-law
and with her husband's other wife, and she had
come to the consul with preposterous questions
about her rights according to Chinese law. He
repeated his offer to get her away, but she remained steadfast in her refusal to go, and their
interview always ended in the consul's flying into a
passion. He was almost inclined to pity the rascally Yü who had to keep the peace between three
warring women. According to his English wife's
account he was not unkind to her. He tried to
act fairly by both his wives. Miss Lambert did

119

not improve. The consul knew that ordinarily she wore Chinese clothes, but when she came to see him she put on European dress. She was become extremely blowsy. Her health suffered from the Chinese food she ate and she was beginning to look wretchedly ill. But really he was shocked when she had been shown into his office that day. She wore no hat and her hair was dishevelled. She was in a highly hysterical state.

"They're trying to poison me," she screamed and she put before him a bowl of some foul smelling food. "It's poisoned," she said. "I've been ill for the last ten days, it's only by a miracle I've escaped."

She gave him a long story, circumstantial and probable enough to convince him: after all nothing was more likely than that the Chinese women should use familiar methods to get rid of an intruder who was hateful to them.

"Do they know you've come here?"

"Of course they do; I told them I was going to show them up."

Now at last was the moment for decisive action. The consul looked at her in his most official manner.

"Well, you must never go back there. I refuse to put up with your nonsense any longer. I insist on your leaving this man who isn't your husband."

But he found himself helpless against the woman's insane obstinacy. He repeated all the arguments he had used so often, but she would not

120

listen, and as usual he lost his temper. It was then, in answer to his final, desperate question, that she had made the remark which had entirely robbed him of his calm.

"But what on earth makes you stay with the man?" he cried.

She hesitated for a moment and a curious look came into her eyes.

"There's something in the way his hair grows on his forehead that I can't help liking," she answered.

The consul had never heard anything so outrageous. It really was the last straw. And now while he strode along, trying to walk off his anger, though he was not a man who often used bad language he really could not restrain himself, and he said fiercely:

"Women are simply bloody."

XXXI

THE STRIPLING

HE walked along the causeway with an easy confident stride. He was seventeen, tall and slim, with a smooth and yellow skin that had never known a razor. His eyes, but slightly aslant, were large and open and his full red lips were tremulous with a smile. The happy audacity of youth was in his bearing. His little round cap was set jauntily on his head, his black gown was girt about his loins, and his trousers, as a rule gartered at the ankle, were turned up to the knees. He went barefoot but for thin straw sandals, and his feet were small and shapely. He had walked since early morning along the paved causeway that wound its sinuous path up the hills and down into the valleys with their innumerable padi fields, past burial grounds with their serried dead, through busy villages where maybe his eyes rested approvingly for a moment on some pretty girl in her blue smock and her short blue trousers, sitting in an open doorway (but I think his glance claimed admiration rather than gave it), and now he was nearing the end of his journey and the city whither he was bound seeking his fortune. It stood in the midst of a fertile plain, surrounded by a crenellated wall, and when he saw it he stepped forward with resolution. He threw back his head boldly. He was proud of his strength. All his worldly goods were wrapped up in a parcel of blue cotton which he carried over his shoulder.

Now Dick Whittington, setting out to win fame and fortune, had a cat for his companion, but the Chinese carried with him a round cage with red bars, which he held with a peculiar grace between finger and thumb, and in the cage was a beautiful green parrot.

XXXII

THE FANNINGS

THEY lived in a fine square house, with a
verandah all round it, on the top of a
low hill that faced the river, and below
them, a little to the right, was another
fine square house which was the customs; and to
this, for he was deputy commissioner, Fanning
went every day. The city was five miles away and
on the river bank was nothing but a small village
which had sprung up to provide the crews of
junks with what gear or food they needed. In
the city were a few missionaries but these they
saw seldom and the only foreigners in the village
besides themselves were the tide-waiters. One of
these had been an able seaman and the other was
an Italian; they both had Chinese wives. The
Fannings asked them to tiffin on Christmas day
and on the King's Birthday; but otherwise their
relations with them were purely official. The
steamers stayed but half an hour, so they never
saw the captains or the chief engineers who were
the only white men on them, and for five months in
the year the water was too low for steamers to
pass. Oddly enough it was then they saw most
foreigners, for it happened now and again that a

traveller, a merchant or consular official perhaps, more often a missionary, going up stream by junk, tied up for the night, and then the commissioner went down to the river and asked him to dine. They lived very much alone.

Fanning was extremely bald, a short, thickset man, with a snub nose and a very black moustache. He was a martinet, aggressive, brusque, with a bullying manner; and he never spoke to a Chinese without raising his voice to a tone of rasping command. Though he spoke fluent Chinese, when one of his "boys" did something to displease him he abused him roundly in English. He made a disagreeable impression on you till you discovered that his aggressiveness was merely an armour put on to conceal a painful shyness. It was a triumph of his will over his disposition. His gruffness was an almost absurd attempt to persuade those with whom he came in contact that he was not frightened of them. You felt that no one was more surprised than himself that he was taken seriously. He was like those little grotesque figures that children blow out like balloons and you had an idea that he went in lively fear of bursting and then everyone would see that he was but a hollow bladder. It was his wife who was constantly alert to persuade him that he was a man of iron and when the explosion was over she would say to him:

"You know, you frighten me when you get in those passions," or "I think I'd better say something to the boy, he's quite shaken by what you said."

Then Fanning would puff himself up and smile indulgently. When a visitor came she would say:

"The Chinese are terrified of my husband, but of course they respect him. They know it's no good trying any of their nonsense with him."

"Well, I ought to know how to treat them," he would answer with beetling brows, "I've been over twenty years in the country."

Mrs. Fanning was a little plain woman, wizened like a crab-apple, with a big nose and bad teeth. She was always very untidy, her hair, going a little grey, was continually on the point of falling down. Now and then, in the midst of conversation, she would abstractedly take out a pin or two, give it a shake, and without troubling to look in the glass insecurely fix its few thin wisps. She had a love of brilliant colour and she wore fantastic clothes which she and the sewing amah ran up together from the fashion papers; but when she dressed she could never find anything that went with anything else and she looked like a woman who had been rescued from shipwreck and clothed in any oddments that could be found. She was a caricature, and you could not help smiling when you looked at her. The only attractive thing she had was a soft and extremely musical voice and she spoke with a little drawl which came from I know not what part of England. The Fannings had two sons, one of nine and one of seven, and they completed the solitary household. They were attractive children, affectionate and demonstrative, and it was pleasant to see how united the

126

family was. They had little jokes together that amused them hugely, and they played pranks with one another as though not one of them was more than ten. Though they had so much of one another's society it really looked as though they could not bear to be out of one another's sight, and each day when Fanning went to his office his boys would hardly let him go and each day when he returned they greeted him with extravagant delight. They had no fear of his gruff bluster.

And presently you discovered that the centre of this concord was that little, grotesque, ugly woman; it was not chance that kept the family united, nor peculiarly agreeable dispositions, but a passion of love in her. From the moment she got up in the morning till the time she went to bed her thoughts were occupied with the welfare of the three male persons who were in her charge. Her active mind was busy all the time with schemes for their happiness. I do not think a thought of self ever entered her untidy head. She was a miracle of unselfishness. It was really hardly human. She never had a hard word for anyone. She was very hospitable and it was she who caused her husband to go down to the houseboats and invite travellers to come up to dinner. But I do not think she wanted them for her own sake. She was quite happy in her solitude, but she thought her husband enjoyed a talk with strangers.

"I don't want him to get in a rut," she said. "My poor husband, he misses his billiards and his bridge. It's very hard for a man to have no one to talk to but a woman."

Every evening when the children had been put to bed they played piquet. She had no head for cards, poor dear, and she always made mistakes, but when her husband upbraided her, she said:

"You can't expect everyone to be as clever as you are."

And because she so obviously meant what she said he could not find it in his heart to be angry with her. Then when the commissioner was tired of beating her they would turn on the gramophone and sitting side by side listen in silence to the latest songs from the musical comedies of London. You may turn up your nose. They lived ten thousand miles away from England and it was their only tie with the home they loved: it made them feel not quite so utterly cut off from civilisation. And presently they would talk of what they would do with the children when they grew up; soon it would be time to send them home to school and perhaps a pang passed through the little woman's gentle heart.

"It'll be hard for you, Bertie, when they go," she said. "But perhaps we shall be moved then to some place where there's a club and then you'll be able to go and play bridge in the evenings."

XXXIII

THE SONG OF THE RIVER

YOU hear it all along the river. You hear it, loud and strong, from the rowers as they urge the junk with its high stern, the mast lashed alongside, down the swift running stream. You hear it from the trackers, a more breathless chaunt, as they pull desperately against the current, half a dozen of them perhaps if they are taking up a wupan, a couple of hundred if they are hauling a splendid junk, its square sail set, over a rapid. On the junk a man stands amidships beating a drum incessantly to guide their efforts, and they pull with all their strength, like men possessed, bent double; and sometimes in the extremity of their travail they crawl on the ground, on all fours, like the beasts of the field. They strain, strain fiercely, against the pitiless might of the stream. The leader goes up and down the line and when he sees one who is not putting all his will into the task he brings down his split bamboo on the naked back. Each one must do his utmost or the labour of all is vain. And still they sing a vehement, eager chaunt, the chaunt of the turbulent waters. I do not know how words can describe what there is in it of effort. It serves to express the straining heart, the breaking muscles, and at the same time the indomitable spirit of man which overcomes the pitiless force of nature. Though the rope may part and the great junk swing back, in the end the rapid will be passed; and at the close of the weary day there is the hearty meal and perhaps the opium pipe with its dreams of ease. But the most agonising song is the song of the coolies who bring the great bales from the junk up the steep steps to the town wall. Up and down they go, endlessly, and endless as their toil rises their rhythmic cry. He, aw—ah, oh. They are barefoot and naked to the waist. The sweat pours down their faces and their song is a groan of pain. It is a sigh of despair. It is heart-rending. It is hardly human. It is the cry of souls in infinite distress, only just musical, and that last note is the ultimate sob of humanity. Life is too hard, too cruel, and this is the final despairing protest. That is the song of the river.

XXXIV

MIRAGE

H E is a tall man with bulging, sky blue eyes and an embarrassed manner. He looks as though he were a little too large for his skin and you feel that he would be more comfortable if it were a trifle looser. His hair, very smooth and crisp, fits so tightly on his head that it gives you the impression of a wig, and you have an almost irresistible inclination to pull it. He has no small talk. He hunts for topics of conversation and, racking his brain to no purpose, in desperation offers you a whisky and soda.

He is in charge of the B. A. T., and the building in which he lives is office, godown, and residence all in one. His parlour is furnished with a suite of dingy upholstered furniture placed neatly round the walls, and in the middle is a round table. A hanging petroleum lamp gives a melancholy light, and an oil stove heat. In appropriate places are richly framed oleographs from the Christmas numbers of American magazines. But he does not sit in this room. He spends his leisure in his bedroom. In America he has always lived in a boarding house where his bedroom was the only privacy he knew, and he has gotten the habit of living in one. It seems unnatural to him to sit in a sitting-room; he does not like to take his coat off, and he only feels at home in shirt sleeves. He keeps his books and his private papers in his bedroom; he has a desk and a rocking chair there.

He has lived in China for five years, but he knows no Chinese and takes no interest in the race among whom in all likelihood the best years of his life will be spent. His business is done through an interpreter and his house is managed by a boy. Now and then he takes a journey of several hundred miles into Mongolia, a wild and rugged country, either in Chinese carts or on ponies; and he sleeps at the wayside inns where congregate merchants, drovers, herdsmen, men at arms, ruffians, and wild fellows. The people of the land are turbulent; when there is unrest he is exposed to not a little risk. But these are purely business undertakings. They bore him. He is always glad to get back to his familiar bedroom at the B. A. T. For he is a great reader. He reads nothing but American magazines and the number of those he has sent to him by every mail is amazing. He never throws them away and there are piles of them all over the house. The city in which he lives is the gateway into China from Mongolia. There dwell the teeming Chinese, and through its gates pass constantly the Mongols with their caravans of camels; endless processions of carts, drawn by oxen, which have brought hides from the illimitable distances of

Asia rumble noisily through its crowded streets. He is bored. It has never occurred to him that he lives a life in which the possibility of adventure is at his doors. He can only recognise it through the printed page; and it needs a story of derring-do in Texas or Nevada, of hairbreadth escape in the South Seas, to stir his blood.

XXXV

THE STRANGER

IT was a comfort in that sweltering heat to get
out of the city. The missionary stepped out
of the launch in which he had dropped leisurely down the river and comfortably settled himself in the chair which was waiting for him
at the water's edge. He was carried through the
village by the river side and began to ascend the
hill. It was an hour's journey along a pathway
of broad stone steps, under fir trees, and now and
again you caught a delightful glimpse of the
broad river shining in the sun amid the exultant
green of the padi fields. The bearers went along
with a swinging stride. The sweat on their backs
shone. It was a sacred mountain with a Buddhist
monastery on the top of it, and on the way up
there were rest houses where the coolies set down
the chair for a few minutes and a monk in his
grey robe gave you a cup of flowered tea. The
air was fresh and sweet. The pleasure of that
lazy journey—the swing of the chair was very
soothing—made a day in the city almost worth
while; and at the end of it was his trim little bungalow where he spent the summer, and before him
the sweet-scented night. The mail had come in

that day and he was bringing on letters and papers. There were four numbers of the *Saturday Evening Post* and four of the *Literary Digest*. He had nothing but pleasant things to look forward to and the usual peace (a peace, as he often said, which passeth all understanding), which filled him whenever he was among these green trees, away from the teeming city, should long since have descended upon him.

But he was harassed. He had had that day an unfortunate encounter and he was unable, trivial as it was, to put it out of his mind. It was on this account that his face bore a somewhat peevish expression. It was a thin and sensitive face, almost ascetic, with regular features and intelligent eyes. He was very long and thin, with the spindly legs of a grasshopper, and as he sat in his chair swaying a little with the motion of his bearers he reminded you, somewhat grotesquely, of a faded lily. A gentle creature. He could never have hurt a fly.

He had run across Dr. Saunders in one of the streets of the city. Dr. Saunders was a little grey-haired man, with a high colour and a snub nose which gave him a strangely impudent expression. He had a large sensual mouth and when he laughed, which he did very often, he showed decayed and discoloured teeth; when he laughed his little blue eyes wrinkled in a curious fashion and then he looked the very picture of malice. There was something faunlike in him. His movements were quick and unexpected. He walked with a

rapid trip as though he were always in a hurry.
He was a doctor who lived in the heart of the city
among the Chinese. He was not on the register,
but someone had made it his business to find out
that he had been duly qualified; he had been struck
off, but for what crime, whether social or purely
professional, none know; nor how he had happened to come to the East and eventually settle on
the China coast. But it was evident that he was a
very clever doctor and the Chinese had great faith
in him. He avoided the foreigners and rather disagreeable stories were circulated about him.
Everyone knew him to say how do you do to, but
no one asked him to his house nor visited him in
his own.

When they had met that afternoon Dr. Saunders
had exclaimed:

"What on earth has brought you to the city
at this time of year?"

"I have some business that I couldn't leave any
longer," answered the missionary, "and then I
wanted to get the mail."

"There was a stranger here the other day asking for you," said the doctor.

"For me?" cried the other with surprise.

"Well, not for you particularly," explained the
doctor. "He wanted to know the way to the
American Mission. I told him; but I said he
wouldn't find anyone there. He seemed rather surprised at that, so I told him that you all went up
to the hills in May and didn't come back till September."

"A foreigner?" asked the missionary, still wondering who the stranger could be.

"Oh, yes, certainly." The doctor's eyes twinkled. "Then he asked me about the other missions; I told him the London Mission had a settlement here, but it wasn't the least use going there as all the missionaries were away in the hills. After all it's devilish hot in the city. 'Then I'd like to go to one of the mission schools,' said the stranger. 'Oh, they're all closed,' I said. 'Well, then I'll go to the hospital.' 'That's well worth a visit,' I said, 'the American hospital is equipped with all the latest contrivances. Their operating theatre is perfect.' 'What is the name of the doctor in charge?' 'Oh, he's up in the hills.' 'But what about the sick?' 'There are no sick between May and September,' I said, 'and if there are they have to put up with the native dispensers.' "

Dr. Saunders paused for a moment. The missionary looked ever so slightly vexed.

"Well?" he said.

"The stranger looked at me irresolutely for a moment or two. 'I wanted to see something of the missions before I left,' he said. 'You might try the Roman Catholics,' I said, 'they're here all the year round.' 'When do they take their holidays then?' he asked. 'They don't,' I said. He left me at that. I think he went to the Spanish convent."

The missionary fell into the trap and it irritated him to think how ingenuously he had done so. He ought to have seen what was coming.

"Who was this anyway?" he asked innocently.

"I asked him his name," said the doctor. 'Oh, I'm Christ,' he said."

The missionary shrugged his shoulders and abruptly told his rickshaw boy to go on.

It had put him thoroughly out of temper. It was so unjust. Of course they went away from May to September. The heat made any useful activity quite out of the question and it had been found by experience that the missionaries preserved their health and strength much better if they spent the hot months in the hills. A sick missionary was only an encumbrance. It was a matter of practical politics and it had been found that the Lord's work was done more efficiently if a certain part of the year was set aside for rest and recreation. And then the reference to the Roman Catholics was grossly unfair. They were unmarried. They had no families to think of. The mortality among them was terrifying. Why, in that very city, of fourteen nuns who had come out to China ten years ago all but three were dead. It was perfectly easy for them, because it was more convenient for their work, to live in the middle of the city and to stay there all the year round. They had no ties. They had no duties to those who were near and dear to them. Oh, it was grossly unjust to drag in the Roman Catholics.

But suddenly an idea flashed through his mind. What rankled most was that he had left the rascally doctor (you only had to look at his face all puckered with malicious amusement to know he was a rogue) without a word. There certainly

138

was an answer, but he had not had the presence of mind to make it; and now the perfect repartee occurred to him. A glow of satisfaction filled him and he almost fancied that he had made it. It was a crushing rejoinder and he rubbed his very long thin hands with satisfaction. 'My dear Sir,' he ought to have said, 'Our Lord never in the whole course of his ministry claimed to be the Christ." It was an unanswerable snub, and thinking of it the missionary forgot his ill-humour.

XXXVI

DEMOCRACY

IT was a cold night. I had finished my dinner, and my boy was making up my bed while I sat over a brazier of burning charcoal. Most of the coolies had already settled themselves for the night in a room next to mine and through the thin matchboarding of the wall that separated us I heard a couple of them talk. Another party of travellers had arrived about an hour before and the small inn was full. Suddenly there was a commotion and going to the door of my room to look out I saw three sedan chairs enter the courtyard. They were set down in front of me and from the first stepped out a stout Chinese of imposing aspect. He wore a long black robe of figured silk, lined with squirrel, and on his head a square fur cap. He seemed taken aback when he saw me at the door of the principal guest chamber and turning to the landlord addressed him in authoritative tones. It appeared that he was an official and he was much annoyed to find that the best apartment in the inn was already taken. He was told that but one room was available. It was small, with pallets covered with tumbled straw lining the walls, and was used as a rule only by

140

coolies. He flung into a violent passion and on a sudden arose a scene of the greatest animation. The official, his two companions, and his bearers exclaimed against the indignity which it was sought to thrust upon him, while the landlord and the servants of the inn argued, expostulated, and entreated. The official stormed and threatened. For a few minutes the courtyard, so silent before, rang with the angry shouts; then, subsiding as quickly as it began, the hubbub ceased and the official went into the vacant room. Hot water was brought by a bedraggled servant, and presently the landlord followed with great bowls of steaming rice. All was once more quiet.

An hour later I went into the yard to stretch my legs for five minutes before going to bed and somewhat to my surprise, I came upon the stout official, a little while ago so pompous and self-important, seated at a table in the front of the inn with the most ragged of my coolies. They were chatting amicably and the official quietly smoked a water-pipe. He had made all that to-do to give himself face, but having achieved his object was satisfied, and feeling the need of conversation had accepted the company of any coolie without a thought of social distinction. His manner was perfectly cordial and there was in it no trace of condescension. The coolie talked with him on an equal footing. It seemed to me that this was true democracy. In the East man is man's equal in a sense you find neither in Europe nor in America. Position and wealth put a man in a

141

relation of superiority to another that is purely adventitious, and they are no bar to sociability.

When I lay in my bed I asked myself why in the despotic East there should be between men an equality so much greater than in the free and democratic West, and was forced to the conclusion that the explanation must be sought in the cess-pool. For in the West we are divided from our fellows by our sense of smell. The working man is our master, inclined to rule us with an iron hand, but it cannot be denied that he stinks: none can wonder at it, for a bath in the dawn when you have to hurry to your work before the factory bell rings is no pleasant thing, nor does heavy labour tend to sweetness; and you do not change your linen more than you can help when the week's washing must be done by a sharp-tongued wife. I do not blame the working man because he stinks, but stink he does. It makes social intercourse difficult to persons of a sensitive nostril. The matutinal tub divides the classes more effectually than birth, wealth, or education. It is very significant that those novelists who have risen from the ranks of labour are apt to make it a symbol of class prejudice, and one of the most distinguished writers of our day always marks the rascals of his entertaining stories by the fact that they take a bath every morning. Now, the Chinese live all their lives in the proximity of very nasty smells. They do not notice them. Their nostrils are blunted to the odours that assail the Europeans and so they can move on an equal footing with the tiller of the soil, the coolie, and the artisan. I venture to think that the cess-pool is more necessary to democracy than parliamentary institutions. The invention of the "sanitary convenience" has destroyed the sense of equality in men. It is responsible for class hatred much more than the monopoly of capital in the hands of the few.

It is a tragic thought that the first man who pulled the plug of a water-closet with that negligent gesture rang the knell of democracy.

XXXVII

THE SEVENTH DAY ADVENTIST

HE was a big man, and his bones were well covered. He gave you the impression that he had put on flesh since he bought his clothes, for they seemed somewhat tight for him. He always wore the same things, a blue suit, evidently bought ready-made in a department store (the lapel decorated with a small American flag) a high starched collar and a white tie on which was a pattern of forget-me-nots. His short nose and pugnacious chin gave his clean-shaven face a determined look; his eyes, behind large, gold-rimmed spectacles, were large and blue; and his hair receding on the temples, lank and dull, was plastered down on his head. But on the crown protruded a rebellious cock's feather.

He was travelling up the Yangtze for the first time, but he took no interest in his surroundings. He had no eye for the waste of turbulent waters that was spread before him, nor for the colours, tragic or tender, which sunrise and sunset lent the scene. The great junks with their square white sails proceeded stately down the stream. The moon rose, flooding the noble river with silver and giving a strange magic to the temples on the bank,

among a grove of trees. He was frankly bored.
During a certain part of the day he studied Chinese, but for the rest of the time he read nothing
but a *New York Times* three months old and the
Parliamentary debates of July, 1915, which,
heaven knows why, happened to be on board. He
took no interest in the religions which flourished
in the land he had come to evangelise. He classed
them all contemptuously as devil worship. I do
not think he had ever read the Analects of Confucius. He was ignorant of the history, art, and
literature of China.

I could not make out what had brought him to
the country. He spoke of his work as a profession which he had entered as a man might enter
the civil service, and which, though it was poorly
paid (he complained that he earned less than an
artisan) he wanted notwithstanding to make a
good job of. He wanted to increase his church
membership, he wanted to make his school self-supporting. If ever he had had a serious call to
convert the heathen there was in him no trace of
it now. He looked upon the whole matter as a
business proposition. The secret of success lay
in the precious word organization. He was upright, honest, and virtuous, but there was neither
passion in him nor enthusiasm. He seemed to be
under the impression that the Chinese were very
simple people, and because they did not know the
same things that he did he thought them ignorant.
He could not help showing that he looked upon
himself as superior to them. The laws they made

K 145

were not applicable to the white man and he resented the fact that they expected him to con-
form to their customs. But he was not a bad fellow; indeed he was a good-humoured one and so
long as you did not attempt to question his authority there is no doubt that he would have done
everything in his power to serve you.

XXXVIII

THE PHILOSOPHER

IT was surprising to find so vast a city in a spot that seemed to me so remote. From its battlemented gate towards sunset you could see the snowy mountains of Tibet. It was so populous that you could walk at ease only on the walls and it took a rapid walker three hours to complete their circuit. There was no railway within a thousand miles and the river on which it stood was so shallow that only junks of light burden could safely navigate it. Five days in a sampan were needed to reach the Upper Yangtze. For an uneasy moment you asked yourself whether trains and steamships were as necessary to the conduct of life as we who use them every day consider; for here, a million persons throve, married, begat their kind, and died; here a million persons were busily occupied with commerce, art, and thought.

And here lived a philosopher of repute the desire to see whom had been to me one of the incentives of a somewhat arduous journey. He was the greatest authority in China on the Confucian learning. He was said to speak English and German with facility. He had been for

many years secretary to one of the Empress Dowager's greatest viceroys, but he lived now in retirement. On certain days in the week, however,
all through the year he opened his doors to such
as sought after knowledge, and discoursed on the
teaching of Confucius. He had a body of disciples, but it was small, since the students for the
most part preferred to his modest dwelling and his
severe exhortations the sumptuous buildings of
the foreign university and the useful science of the
barbarians: with him this was mentioned only to
be scornfully dismissed. From all I heard of him
I concluded that he was a man of character.

When I announced my wish to meet this distinguished person my host immediately offered to
arrange a meeting; but the days passed and
nothing happened. I made enquiries and my host
shrugged his shoulders.

"I sent him a chit and told him to come along,"
he said. "I don't know why he hasn't turned up.
He's a cross-grained old fellow."

I did not think it was proper to approach a
philosopher in so cavalier a fashion and I was
hardly surprised that he had ignored a summons
such as this. I caused a letter to be sent asking
in the politest terms I could devise whether he
would allow me to call upon him and within two
hours received an answer making an appointment
for the following morning at ten o'clock.

I was carried in a chair. The way seemed interminable. I went through crowded streets and
through streets deserted till I came at last to one,

148

silent and empty, in which at a small door in a
long white wall my bearers set down my chair.
One of them knocked, and after a considerable
time a judas was opened; dark eyes looked
through; there was a brief colloquy; and finally
I was admitted. A youth, pallid of face, wizened,
and poorly dressed, motioned me to follow him. I
did not know if he was a servant or a pupil of the
great man. I passed through a shabby yard and
was led into a long low room sparsely furnished
with an American roll-top desk, a couple of black-
wood chairs and two little Chinese tables. Against
the walls were shelves on which were a great number of books: most of them, of course, were Chinese, but there were many, philosophical and sci-
entific works, in English, French and German;
and there were hundreds of unbound copies of
learned reviews. Where books did not take up the
wall space hung scrolls on which in various calligraphies were written, I suppose, Confucian quo-
tations. There was no carpet on the floor. It
was a cold, bare, and comfortless chamber. Its
sombreness was relieved only by a yellow chrysanthemum which stood by itself on the desk in a long
vase.

I waited for some time and the youth who had
shown me in brought a pot of tea, two cups, and
a tin of Virginian cigarettes. As he went out the
philosopher entered. I hastened to express my
sense of the honour he did me in allowing me to
visit him. He waved me to a chair and poured out
the tea.

"I am flattered that you wished to see me," he returned. "Your countrymen deal only with coolies and with compradores; they think every Chinese must be one or the other."

I ventured to protest. But I had not caught his point. He leaned back in his chair and looked at me with an expression of mockery.

"They think they have but to beckon and we must come."

I saw then that my friend's unfortunate communication still rankled. I did not quite know how to reply. I murmured something complimentary.

He was an old man, tall, with a thin grey queue, and bright large eyes under which were heavy bags. His teeth were broken and discoloured. He was exceedingly thin, and his hands, fine and small, were withered and claw-like. I had been told that he was an opium-smoker. He was very shabbily dressed in a black gown, a little black cap, both much the worse for wear, and dark grey trousers gartered at the ankle. He was watching. He did not quite know what attitude to take up, and he had the manner of a man who was on his guard. Of course the philosopher occupies a royal place among those who concern themselves with the things of the spirit and we have the authority of Benjamin Disraeli that royalty must be treated with abundant flattery. I seized my trowel. Presently I was conscious of a certain relaxation in his demeanour. He was like a man who was all set and rigid to have his photograph taken, but

150

hearing the shutter click lets himself go and eases into his natural self. He showed me his books.

"I took the Ph. D. in Berlin, you know," he said. "And afterwards I studied for some time in Oxford. But the English, if you will allow me to say so, have no great aptitude for philosophy."

Though he put the remark apologetically it was evident that he was not displeased to say a slightly disagreeable thing.

"We have had philosophers who have not been without influence in the world of thought," I suggested.

"Hume and Berkeley? The philosophers who taught at Oxford when I was there were anxious not to offend their theological colleagues. They would not follow their thought to its logical consequences in case they should jeopardise their position in university society.

"Have you studied the modern developments of philosophy in America?" I asked.

"Are you speaking of Pragmatism? It is the last refuge of those who want to believe the incredible. I have more use for American petroleum than for American philosophy."

His judgments were tart. We sat down once more and drank another cup of tea. He began to talk with fluency. He spoke a somewhat formal but an idiomatic English. Now and then he helped himself out with a German phrase. So far as it was possible for a man of that stubborn character to be influenced he had been influenced by Germany. The method and the industry of the Germans had deeply impressed him and their philosophical acumen was patent to him when a laborious professor published in a learned magazine an essay on one of his own writings.

"I have written twenty books," he said. "And that is the only notice that has ever been taken of me in a European publication."

But his study of Western philosophy had only served in the end to satisfy him that wisdom after all was to be found within the limits of the Confucian canon. He accepted its philosophy with conviction. It answered the needs of his spirit with a completeness which made all foreign learning seem vain. I was interested in this because it bore out an opinion of mine that philosophy is an affair of character rather than of logic: the philosopher believes not according to evidence, but according to his own temperament; and his thinking merely serves to make reasonable what his instinct regards as true. If Confucianism gained so firm a hold on the Chinese it is because it explained and expressed them as no other system of thought could do.

My host lit a cigarette. His voice at first had been thin and tired, but as he grew interested in what he said it gained volume. He talked vehemently. There was in him none of the repose of the sage. He was a polemist and a fighter. He loathed the modern cry for individualism. For him society was the unit, and the family the foundation of society. He upheld the old China and the old school, monarchy, and the rigid canon of

Confucius. He grew violent and bitter as he spoke of the students, fresh from foreign universities, who with sacrilegious hands tore down the oldest civilisation in the world.

"But you, do you know what you are doing?" he exclaimed. "What is the reason for which you deem yourselves our betters? Have you excelled us in arts or letters? Have our thinkers been less profound than yours? Has our civilisation been less elaborate, less complicated, less refined than yours? Why, when you lived in caves and clothed yourselves with skins we were a cultured people. Do you know that we tried an experiment which is unique in the history of the world? We sought to rule this great country not by force, but by wisdom. And for centuries we succeeded. Then why does the white man despise the yellow? Shall I tell you? Because he has invented the machine gun. That is your superiority. We are a defenceless horde and you can blow us into eternity. You have shattered the dream of our philosophers that the world could be governed by the power of law and order. And now you are teaching our young men your secret. You have thrust your hideous inventions upon us. Do you not know that we have a genius for mechanics? Do you not know that there are in this country four hundred millions of the most practical and industrious people in the world? Do you think it will take us long to learn? And what will become of your superiority when the yellow man can make as good guns as the white and fire them as

153

straight? You have appealed to the machine gun
and by the machine gun shall you be judged."

But at that moment we were interrupted. A
little girl came softly in and nestled close up to
the old gentleman. She stared at me with curious
eyes. He told me that she was his youngest child.
He put his arms round her and with a murmur of
caressing words kissed her fondly. She wore a
black coat and trousers that barely reached her
ankles, and she had a long pig-tail hanging down
her back. She was born on the day the revolution was brought to a successful issue by the abdi-
cation of the emperor.

"I thought she heralded the Spring of a new
era," he said. "She was but the last flower of
this great nation's Fall."

From a drawer in his roll-top desk he took a
few cash, and handing them to her, sent her away.

"You see that I wear a queue," he said, taking
it in his hands. "It is a symbol. I am the last
representative of the old China."

He talked to me, more gently now, of how philosophers in long past days wandered from state
to state with their disciples, teaching all who were
worthy to learn. Kings called them to their coun-
cils and made them rulers of cities. His erudition
was great and his eloquent phrases gave a multi-
coloured vitality to the incidents he related to me
of the history of his country. I could not help
thinking him a somewhat pathetic figure. He felt
in himself the capacity to administer the state,
but there was no king to entrust him with office;

he had vast stores of learning which he was eager
to impart to the great band of students that his
soul hankered after, and there came to listen but
a few, wretched, half-starved, and obtuse pro-
vincials.

Once or twice discretion had made me suggest
that I should take my leave, but he had been unwilling to let me go. Now at last I was obliged
to. I rose. He held my hand.

"I should like to give you something as a recollection of your visit to the last philosopher in
China, but I am a poor man and I do not know
what I can give you that would be worthy of your
acceptance."

I protested that the recollection of my visit was
in itself a priceless gift. He smiled.

"Men have short memories in these degenerate
days, and I should like to give you something more
substantial. I would give you one of my books,
but you cannot read Chinese."

He looked at me with an amicable perplexity.
I had an inspiration.

"Give me a sample of your calligraphy," I
said.

"Would you like that?" He smiled. "In my
youth I was considered to wield the brush in a
manner that was not entirely despicable."

He sat down at his desk, took a fair sheet of
paper, and placed it before him. He poured a
few drops of water on a stone, rubbed the ink
stick in it, and took his brush. With a free movement of the arm he began to write. And as I

watched him I remembered with not a little amusement something else which had been told me of him. It appeared that the old gentleman, whenever he could scrape a little money together, spent it wantonly in the streets inhabited by ladies to describe whom a euphemism is generally used. His eldest son, a person of standing in the city, was vexed and humiliated by the scandal of this behaviour; and only his strong sense of filial duty prevented him from reproaching the libertine with severity. I daresay that to a son such looseness would be disconcerting, but the student of human nature could look upon it with equanimity. Philosophers are apt to elaborate their theories in the study, forming conclusions upon life which they know only at second hand, and it has seemed to me often that their works would have a more definite significance if they had exposed themselves to the vicissitudes which befall the common run of men. I was prepared to regard the old gentleman's dalliance in hidden places with leniency. Perhaps he sought but to elucidate the most inscrutable of human illusions.

He finished. To dry the ink he scattered a little ash on the paper and rising handed it to me.

"What have you written?" I asked.

I thought there was a slightly malicious gleam in his eyes.

"I have ventured to offer you two little poems of my own."

"I did not know you were a poet."

"When China was still an uncivilised country,"

he retorted with sarcasm, "all educated men could write verse at least with elegance."

I took the paper and looked at the Chinese characters. They made an agreeable pattern upon it.

"Won't you also give me a translation?"

"*Tradutore—tradittore,*" he answered. "You cannot expect me to betray myself. Ask one of your English friends. Those who know most about China know nothing, but you will at least find one who is competent to give you a rendering of a few rough and simple lines."

I bade him farewell, and with great politeness he showed me to my chair. When I had the opportunity I gave the poems to a sinologue of my acquaintance, and here is the version he made.[1] I confess that, doubtless unreasonably, I was somewhat taken aback when I read it.

You loved me not: your voice was sweet;
Your eyes were full of laughter; your hands were
tender.
And then you loved me: your voice was bitter;
Your eyes were full of tears; your hands were cruel.
Sad, sad that love should make you
Unlovable.

———

I craved the years would quickly pass
That you might lose
The brightness of your eyes, the peach-bloom of your
skin,
And all the cruel splendour of your youth.
Then I alone would love you
And you at last would care.

[1] I owe it to the kindness of my friend Mr. P. W. Davidson.

The envious years have passed full soon
And you have lost
The brightness of your eyes, the peach-bloom of
your skin,
And all the charming splendour of your youth.
Alas, I do not love you
And I care not if you care.

XXXIX

THE MISSIONARY LADY

SHE was certainly fifty, but a life of convictions harassed by never a doubt had left her face unwrinkled. The hesitations of thought had never lined the smoothness of her brow. Her features were bold and regular, somewhat masculine, and her determined chin bore out the impression given you by her eyes. They were blue, confident, and unperturbed. They summed you up through large round spectacles. You felt that here was a woman to whom command came easily. Her charity was above all things competent and you were certain that she ran the obvious goodness of her heart on thoroughly business lines. It was possible to suppose that she was not devoid of human vanity (and this is to be counted to her for grace) since she wore a dress of violet silk, heavily embroidered, and a toque of immense pansies which on a less respectable head would have been almost saucy. But my Uncle Henry, for twenty-seven years Vicar of Whitstable, who had decided views on the proper manner of dress for a clergyman's wife, never objected to my Aunt Sophie wearing violet, and he would have found nothing to criticise in

159

the missionary lady's gown. She spoke fluently with the even flow of water turned on at a tap. Her conversation had the admirable volubility of a politician at the end of an electioneering campaign. You felt that she knew what she meant (with most of us so rare an accomplishment) and meant what she said.

"I always think," she remarked pleasantly, "that if you know both sides of a question you'll judge differently from what you will if you only know one side. But the fact remains that two and two make four and you can argue all night and you won't make them five. Am I right or am I wrong?"

I hastened to assure her that she was right, though with these new theories of relativity and parallel lines behaving at infinity in such a surprising manner I was in my heart of hearts none too sure.

"No one can eat their cake and have it," she continued, exemplifying Benedetto Croce's theory that grammar has little to do with expression, "and one has to take the rough with the smooth, but as I always say to the children you can't expect to have everything your own way. No one is perfect in this world and I always think that if you expect the best from people you'll get the best."

I confess that I was staggered, but I determined to do my part. It was only civil.

"Most men live long enough to discover that every cloud has a silver lining," I began earnestly.

160

"With perseverance you can do most things that are not beyond your powers, and after all, it's better to want what you have than to have what you want."

I thought her eyes were glazed with a sudden perplexity when I made this confident statement, but I daresay it was only my fancy, for she nodded vigorously.

"Of course, I see your point," she said. "We can't do more than we can."

But my blood was up now and I waved aside the interruption. I went on.

"Few people realise the profound truth that there are twenty shillings in every pound and twelve pence in every shilling. I'm sure it's better to see clearly to the end of your nose than indistinctly through a brick wall. If there's one thing we can be certain about it is that the whole is greater than the part."

When, with a hearty shake of the hand, firm and characteristic, she bade me farewell, she said:

"Well, we've had a most interesting chat. It does one good in a place like this, so far away from civilisation, to exchange ideas with one's intellectual equals."

"Especially other people's," I murmured.

"I always think that one should profit by the great thoughts of the past," she retorted. "It shows that the mighty dead have not lived in vain."

Her conversation was devastating.

XL

A GAME OF BILLIARDS

I WAS sitting in the lobby of the hotel, reading a number, several days old, of the *South China Times*, when the door of the bar was somewhat brusquely thrown open and a very long, thin man appeared.

"Do you care for a game of billiards?" he said.

"By all means."

I got up and went with him into the bar. It was a small hotel, of stone, somewhat pretentious in appearance, and it was kept by a half-caste Portuguese who smoked opium. There were not half a dozen people staying there, a Portuguese official and his wife waiting for a ship to take them to a distant colony, a Lancashire engineer who was sullenly drunk all day long, a mysterious lady, no longer young but of voluptuous appearance, who came to the dining room for meals and went back to her room immediately afterwards, and I had not seen the stranger before. I supposed he had come in that evening on a Chinese boat. He was a man of over fifty, I should think, shrivelled as though the sap had been dried out of him by tropical suns, with a face that was almost brick red. I could not place him. He might have been a skipper out of a job or the agent of some foreign firm in Hong Kong. He was very silent and he made no answer to the casual remarks that I made in the course of the game. He played billiards well enough, though not excellently, but he was a very pleasant fellow to play with; and when he pocketed my ball, instead of leaving me a double balk, gave me a reasonable shot. But when the game was over I should never have thought of him again, if suddenly, breaking his silence for the first time, he had not put me a very odd question.

"Do you believe in fate?" he asked.

"At billiards?" I retorted not a little astonished at his remark.

"No, in life."

I did not want to answer him seriously.

"I hardly know," I said.

He took his shot. He made a little break. At the end of it, chalking his cue, he said:

"I do. I believe if things are coming to you, you can't escape them."

That was all. He said nothing more. When we had finished the game he went up to bed, and I never saw him again. I shall never know what strange emotion impelled him to put that sudden question to a stranger.

XLI

THE SKIPPER

I KNEW he was drunk.

He was a skipper of the new school, a neat little man, clean-shaven, who might easily have passed for the commander of a submarine. In his cabin there hung a beautiful new coat with gold braid on it, the uniform which for its good service in the war has been granted to the mercantile marine, but he was shy of using it; it seemed absurd when he was no more than captain of a small boat on the Yangtze; and he stood on his bridge in a neat brown suit and a homburg hat; you could almost see yourself in his admirably polished shoes. His eyes were clear and bright and his skin was fresh. Though he had been at sea for twenty years and could not have been much less than forty he did not look more than twenty-eight. You might be sure that he was a clean-living fellow, as healthy in mind as he was in body, and the depravity of the East of which they talk had left him untouched. He had a pleasant taste in light literature and the works of E. V. Lucas adorned his book-case. In his cabin you saw a photograph of a football team in which he figured and two of a young woman

with neatly waved hair whom it was possible
enough he was engaged to.

I knew he was drunk, but I did not think he
was very drunk, till he asked me suddenly:

"What is democracy?"

I returned an evasive, perhaps a flippant answer, and for some minutes the conversation
turned on less unseasonable topics to the occasion. Then breaking his silence, he said:

"I hope you don't think I'm a socialist because
I said, what is democracy."

"Not at all," I answered, "but I don't see why
you shouldn't be a socialist."

"I give you my word of honour I'm not," he
protested. "If I had my way I'd stand them
up against a wall and shoot them."

"What is socialism?" I asked.

"Oh, you know what I mean, Henderson and
Ramsay Macdonald and all that sort of thing,"
he answered. "I'm about fed up with the working
man."

"But you're a working man yourself, I should
have thought."

He was silent for quite a long time and I thought
his mind had wandered to other things. But I
was wrong; he was thinking my statement over
in all its bearings, for at last he said:

"Look here, I'm not a working man. Hang it
all, I was at Harrow."

XLII

THE SIGHTS OF THE TOWN

I AM not an industrious sight-seer, and when guides, professional or friendly, urge me to visit a famous monument I have a stubborn inclination to send them about their business. Too many eyes before mine have looked with awe upon Mont Blanc; too many hearts before mine have throbbed with deep emotion in the presence of the Sistine Madonna. Sights like these are like women of too generous sympathies: you feel that so many persons have found solace in their commiseration that you are embarrassed when they bid you, with what practised tact, to whisper in their discreet ears the whole tale of your distress. Supposing you were the last straw that broke the camel's back! No, Madam, I will take my sorrows (if I cannot bear them alone, which is better) to someone who is not quite so certain of saying so exactly the right thing to comfort me. When I am in a foreign town I prefer to wander at random and if maybe I lose the rapture of a Gothic cathedral I may happen upon a little Romanesque chapel or a Renaissance doorway which I shall be able to flatter myself no one else has troubled about.

But of course this was a very extraordinary sight indeed and it would have been absurd to miss it. I came across it by pure chance. I was sauntering along a dusty road outside the city wall and by the side of it I saw a number of memorial arches. They were small and undecorated, standing not across the way but along it, close to one another, and sometimes one in front of the other, as though they had been erected by no impulse of gratitude to the departed or of admiration for the virtuous but in formal compliment, as knighthoods on the King's birthday are conferred on prominent citizens of provincial towns. Behind this row of arches the land rose sharply and since in this part of the country the Chinese bury their dead by preference on the side of a hill it was thickly covered with graves. A trodden path led to a little tower and I followed it. It was a stumpy little tower, ten feet high perhaps, made of rough-hewn blocks of stone; it was cone shaped and the roof was like a Pierrot's hat. It stood on a hillock, quaint and rather picturesque against the blue sky, amid the graves. At its foot were a number of rough baskets thrown about in disorder. I walked round and on one side saw an oblong hole, eighteen inches by eight, perhaps, from which hung a stout string. From the hole there came a very strange, a nauseating odour. Suddenly I understood what the queer little building was. It was a baby tower. The baskets were the baskets in which the babies had been brought, two or three of them were quite new, they could

167

not have been there more than a few hours. And
the string? Why, if the person who brought the
baby, parent or grandmother, midwife or obliging
friend, were of a humane disposition and did not
care to let the new-born child drop to the bottom
(for underneath the tower was a deep pit), it
could be let down gently by means of the string.
The odour was the odour of putrefaction. A
lively little boy came up to me while I stood there
and made me understand that four babes had
been brought to the tower that morning.

There are philosophers who look upon evil with
a certain complacency, since without it, they
opine, there would be no possibility of good.
Without want there would be no occasion for charity, without distress of sympathy, without danger
of courage, and without unhappiness of resigna-
tion. They would find in the Chinese practice of
infanticide an apt illustration of their views. Ex-
cept for the baby tower there would not be in this
city an orphanage: the traveller would miss an
interesting and curious sight, and a few poor
women would have no opportunity to exercise a
beautiful and touching virtue. The orphanage is
shabby and bedraggled; it is situated in a poor
and crowded part of the city; for the Spanish
nuns who conduct it—there are but five of them
—think it more convenient to live where they may
be most useful; and besides, they have not the
money to build commodious premises in a salubri-
ous quarter. The institution is supported by the

work, lace and fine embroidery, which they teach the girls to do, and by the alms of the faithful.

Two nuns, the Mother Superior and another, showed me what there was to see. It was very strange to go through the whitewashed rooms, work-rooms, playrooms, dormitories, and refectory, low, cool, and bare; for you might have been in Spain, and when you passed a window you half expected to catch a glimpse of the Giralda. And it was charming to see the tenderness with which the nuns used the children. There were two hundred of them and they were, of course, orphans only in the sense that their parents had abandoned them. There was one room in which a number were playing, all of the same age, perhaps four, and all of the same size; with their black eyes and black hair, their yellow skins, they all looked so much alike that they might have been the children of a Chinese Old Woman who lived in a Shoe. They crowded round the nuns and began to romp with them. The Mother Superior had the gentlest voice I ever heard, but it became gentler still when she joked with the tiny mites. They nestled about her. She looked a very picture of charity. Some were deformed and some were diseased, some were puny and hideous, some were blind; it gave me a little shudder: I marvelled when I saw the love that filled her kind eyes and the affectionate sweetness of her smile.

Then I was taken into a parlour where I was made to eat little sweet Spanish cakes and given a glass of Manzanilla to drink, and when I told them that I had lived in Seville a third nun was sent for, so that she might talk for a few minutes with someone who had seen the city she was born in. With pride they showed me their poor little chapel with its tawdry statue of the Blessed Virgin, its paper flowers, and its gaudy, shoddy decoration; for those dear faithful hearts, alas! were possessed of singularly bad taste. I did not care: to me there was something positively touching in that dreadful vulgarity. And when I was on the point of leaving the Mother Superior asked me whether I would care to see the babies who had come in that day. In order to persuade people to bring them they gave twenty cents for every one. Twenty cents!

"You see," she explained, "they have often a long walk to come here and unless we give them something they won't take the trouble."

She took me into a little anteroom, near the entrance, and there lying on a table under a counterpane were four new-born babes. They had just been washed and put into long clothes. The counterpane was lifted off. They lay side by side, on their backs, four tiny wriggling mites, very red in the face, rather cross perhaps because they had been bathed, and very hungry. Their eyes seemed preternaturally large. They were so small, so helpless: you were forced to smile when you looked at them and at the same time you felt a lump in your throat.

XLIII

NIGHTFALL

TOWARDS evening perhaps, tired of walking, you get into your chair and on the crest of a hill you pass through a stone gateway. You cannot tell why there should be a gateway in that deserted spot, far from a village, but a fragment of massive wall suggests the ruin of fortifications against the foes of a forgotten dynasty. And when you come through the gateway you see below you the shining water in the rice fields, diapered, like the chessboard in some Chinese *Alice in Wonderland*, and then the rounded, tree-clad hills. But making your way down the stone steps of the narrow causeway which is the high road from city to city, in the gathering darkness you pass a coppice, and from it waft towards you chill woodland odours of the night. Then you hear no longer the measured tread of your bearers, your ears are on a sudden deaf to their sharp cries as they change the pole from shoulder to shoulder, and to the ceaseless chatter or the occasional snatch of song with which they enliven the monotonous way, for the woodland odours are the same as those which steal up from the fat Kentish soil when you pass

171

through the woods of Bleane; and nostalgia seizes you. Your thoughts travel through time and space, far from the Here and Now, and you remember your vanished youth with its high hopes, its passionate love, and its ambition. Then if you are a cynic, as they say, and therefore a sentimentalist, tears come to your unwilling eyes. And when you have regained your self-control the night has fallen.

XLIV

THE NORMAL MAN

I WAS once obliged to study anatomy, a very
dreary business, since there is neither rhyme
nor reason for the vast number of things
you have to remember; but one remark made
by my teacher, when he was helping me in the dis-
section of a thigh, has always remained in my
memory. I was looking in vain for a certain nerve
and it needed his greater skill to discover it in a
place in which I had not sought it. I was ag-
grieved because the text book had misled me. He
smiled and said:

"You see, the normal is the rarest thing in the
world."

And though he spoke of anatomy he might have
spoken with equal truth of man. The casual observation impressed itself upon me as many a pro-
founder one has not and all the years that have
passed since then, with the increasing knowledge
of human nature which they have brought, have
only strengthened my conviction of its truth. I
have met a hundred men who seemed perfectly
normal only to find in them presently an idiosyn-
crasy so marked as to put them almost in a class
by themselves. It has entertained me not a little

173

to discover the hidden oddity of men to all appearances most ordinary. I have been often amazed to come upon a hideous depravity in men who you would have sworn were perfectly commonplace. I have at last sought the normal man as a precious work of art. It has seemed to me that to know him would give me that peculiar satisfaction which can only be described as æsthetic.

I really thought I had found him in Robert Webb. He was a consul in one of the smaller ports and I was given a letter to him. I heard a good deal about him on my way through China and I heard nothing but good. Whenever I happened to mention that I was going to the port in which he was stationed someone was sure to say:

"You'll like Bob Webb. He's an awfully good chap."

He was no less popular as an official than he was as a private person. He managed to please the merchants because he was active in their interests, without antagonising the Chinese who praised his firmness or the missionaries who approved his private life. During the revolution by his tact, decision, and courage he had not only saved from great danger the foreign population of the city in which he then was, but also many Chinese. He had come forward as a peacemaker between the warring parties and by his ingenuity had been able to bring about a satisfactory settlement. He was marked down for promotion. I certainly found him a very engaging fellow. Though he was not good-looking his appearance was pleasing;

he was tall, perhaps a little more than of average
height, well covered without being fat, with a fresh
complexion inclined now (for he was nearly fifty)
to be somewhat bloated in the morning. This was
not strange, for in China the foreigners both eat
and drink a great deal too much, and Robert Webb
had a healthy liking for the good things of life.
He kept an excellent table. He liked eating in
company and it was seldom that he did not have
one or two people to tiffin or to dinner with him.
His eyes were blue and friendly. He had the social
gifts that give pleasure: he played the piano quite
well, but he liked the music that other people
liked, and he was always ready to play a one step
or a waltz if others wanted to dance. With a wife,
a son, and a daughter in England he could not
afford to keep racing ponies, but he was keenly
interested in racing; he was a good tennis player,
and his bridge was better than the average. Un-
like many of his colleagues he did not allow himself
to be overwhelmed by his position, and in the evening at the club he was affable and unaffected.
But he did not forget that he was His Britannic
Majesty's Consul and I admired the skill with
which without portentousness he preserved the dignity which he thought necessary to his station.
In short he had very good manners. He talked
agreeably, and his interests, though somewhat ordinary, were varied. He had a nice sense of
humour. He could make a joke and tell a good
story. He was very happily married. His son
was at Charterhouse and he showed me a photo-

graph of a tall, fair lad in flannels, with a frank
and pleasant face. He showed me also the photograph of his daughter. It is one of the tragedies
of life in China that a man must be separated for
long periods from his family, and owing to the
war Robert Webb had not seen his for eight years.
His wife had taken the children home when the boy
was eight and the girl eleven. They had meant to
wait till his leave came so that they could go all
together, but he was stationed in a place that
suited neither of the children and he and his wife
agreed that she had better take them at once. His
leave was due in three years and then he could
spend twelve months with them. But when the time
for this came the war broke out, the Consular staff
was short-handed, and it was impossible for him to
leave his post. His wife did not want to be separated from young children, the journey was difficult and dangerous, no one expected the war to
last so long, and one by one the years passed.

"My girl was a child when I saw her last," he
said to me when he showed me the photograph.
"Now she's a married woman."

"When are you going on leave?" I asked him.

"Oh, my wife's coming out now."

"But don't you want to see your daughter?"
I asked.

He looked at the photograph again and then
looked away. There was a curious look in his
face, a somewhat peevish look, I thought, and he
answered:

"I've been away from home too long now. I
shall never go back."

I leaned back in my chair, smoking my pipe.
The photograph showed me a girl of nineteen with
wide blue eyes and bobbed hair; it was a pretty
face, open and friendly, but the most noticeable
thing about it was a peculiar charm of expression. Bob Webb's daughter was a very alluring
young person. I liked that engaging audacity.

"It was rather a surprise to me when she sent
along that photograph," he said presently. "I'd
always thought of her as a child. If I'd met her
in the street I shouldn't have known her."

He gave a little laugh that was not quite natural.

"It isn't fair. . . . When she was a child she
used to love being petted."

His eyes were fixed on the photograph. I
seemed to see in them a very unexpected emotion.

"I can hardly realise she's my daughter. I
thought she'd come back with her mother, and
then she wrote and said she was engaged."

He looked away now and I thought there was a
singular embarrassment in the down-turned corners of his mouth.

"I suppose one gets selfish out here, I felt awfully sore, but I gave a big dinner party to all the
fellows here the day she was married, and we all
got blind."

He gave an apologetic laugh.

"I had to, you know," he said awkwardly. "I
had such an awful hump."

M   177

"What's the young man like?" I asked.

"She's awfully in love with him. When she writes to me her letters are about nothing else." There was an odd quaver in his voice. "It's a bit thick to bring a child into the world and to educate her and be fond of her and all that sort of thing just for some man whom you've never even seen. I've got his photograph somewhere, I don't know where it is. I don't think I'd care about him very much."

He helped himself to another whisky. He was tired. He looked old and bloated. He said nothing for a long time, and then suddenly he seemed to pull himself together.

"Well, thank God, her mother's coming out soon."

I don't think he was quite a normal man after all.

XLV

THE OLD TIMER

HE was seventy-six years old. He had
come to China when he was little more
than a boy as second mate of a sailing
vessel and had never gone home again.
Since then he had been many things. For long
years he had commanded a Chinese boat that ran
from Shanghai to Ichang and he knew by heart
every inch of the great and terrible Yangtze. He
had been master of a tug at Hong-Kong and had
fought in the Ever-Victorious Army. He had got
a lot of loot in the Boxer troubles and had been
in Hankow during the revolution when the rebels
shelled the city. He had been married three times,
first to a Japanese woman, then to a Chinese, and
finally when he was hard upon fifty to an Englishwoman. They were all dead now and it was the
Japanese who lingered in his memory. He would
tell you how she arranged the flowers in the house
in Shanghai, just one chrysanthemum in a vase
or a sprig of cherry blossom; and he always remembered how she held a tea-cup, with both hands,
delicately. He had had a number of children, but
he took no interest in them; they were settled in
the various ports of China, in banks and shipping

179

offices, and he seldom saw them. He was proud of his daughter by his English wife, the only girl he ever had, but she had married well and was gone to England. He would never see her again. The only person now for whom he had any affection was the boy who had been with him for five and forty years. He was a little wizened Chinaman, with a bald head, slow of movement and solemn. He was well over sixty. They quarrelled incessantly. The old timer would tell the boy that he was past his work and that he must get rid of him, and then the boy would say that he was tired of serving a mad foreign devil. But each knew that the other did not mean a word he said. They were old friends, old men both of them, and they would remain together till death parted them.

It was when he married his English wife that he retired from the water and put his savings into a hotel. But it was not a success. It was a little way from Shanghai, a summer resort, and it was before there were motor cars in China. He was a sociable fellow and he spent too much of his time in the bar. He was generous and he gave away as many drinks as were paid for. He also had the peculiar habit of spitting in the bath and the more squeamish of his visitors objected to it. When his last wife died he found it was she who had kept things from going to pieces and in a little while he could no longer bear up against the difficulty of his circumstances. All his savings had gone into buying the place, now heavily mortgaged, and in making up the deficit year by year. He was

obliged to sell out to a Japanese and having paid
his debts at the age of sixty-eight found himself without a penny. But, by God, sir, he was a
sailor. One of the companies running boats up
the Yangtze, gave him a berth as chief officer—he
had no master's certificate—and he returned to
the river which he knew so well. For eight years
he had been on the same run.

And now he stood on the bridge of his trim little
ship, not so large as a penny steamer on the
Thames, a gallant figure, upright and slender as
when he was a lad, in a neat blue suit and the company's cap set jauntily on his white hair, with
his pointed beard nattily trimmed. Seventy-six
years old. It is a great age. With his head
thrown back, his glasses in his hand, the Chinese
pilot by his side, he watched the vast expanse of
the winding river. A fleet of junks with their
high sterns, their square sails set, descended on
the swift current, and the rowers chanted a monotonous chant as they worked at their creaking
oars. The yellow water in the setting sun was
lovely with pale soft tints, it was as smooth as
glass; and along the flat banks the trees and the
huts of a bedraggled village, hazy in the heat of
the day, were now silhouetted sharply, like the
shadows of a shadowgraph, against the pale sky.
He raised his head as he heard the cry of wild
geese and he saw them flying high above him in a
great V to what far lands he knew not. In the
distance against the sunlight stood a solitary
hill crowned with temples. Because he had seen

all this so often it affected him strangely. The dying day made him think, he knew not why, of his long past and of his great age. He regretted nothing.

"By George," he muttered, "I've had a fine life."

XLVI

THE PLAIN

THE incident was of course perfectly trivial, and it could be very easily explained; but I was surprised that the eyes of the spirit could blind me so completely to what was visible to the eyes of sense. I was taken aback to find how completely one could be at the mercy of the laws of association. Day after day I had marched among the uplands and to-day I knew that I must come to the great plain in which lay the ancient city whither I was bound; but when I set out in the morning there was no sign that I approached it. Indeed the hills seemed no less sheer and when I reached the top of one, thinking to see the valley below, it was only to see before me one steeper and taller yet. Beyond, climbing steadily, I could see the white causeway that I had followed so long, shining in the sunlight as it skirted the brow of a rugged tawny rock. The sky was blue and in the west hung here and there little clouds like fishing boats becalmed towards evening off Dungeness. I trudged along, mounting all the time, alert for the prospect that awaited me, if not round this bend, then round the next, and at last, suddenly, when I was thinking

of other things, I came upon it. But it was no
Chinese landscape that I saw, with its padi fields,
its memorial arches and its fantastic temples, with
its farmhouses set in a bamboo grove and its way-
side inns where under the banyan trees the poor
coolies may rest them of their weary loads; it
was the valley of the Rhine, the broad plain all
golden in the sunset, the valley of the Rhine with
its river, a silvery streak, running through it, and
the distant towers of Worms; it was the great
plain upon which my young eyes rested, when, a
student in Heidelberg, after walking long among
the fir-clad hills above the old city, I came out
upon a clearing. And because I was there first
conscious of beauty; because there I knew the first
glow of the acquisition of knowledge (each book
I read was an extraordinary adventure); because
there I first knew the delight of conversation (oh,
those wonderful commonplaces which each boy
discovers as though none had discovered them before); because of the morning stroll in the sunny
Anlage, the cakes and coffee which refreshed my
abstemious youth at the end of a strenuous walk,
the leisurely evenings on the castle terrace, with
the smoky blue haze over the tumbled roofs of the
old town below me; because of Goethe and Heine
and Beethoven and Wagner and (why not?)
Strauss with his waltzes, and the beer-garden
where the band played and girls with yellow plaits
walked sedately; because of all these things—
recollections which have all the force of the appeal
of sense—to me not only does the word *plain* mean

everywhere and exclusively the valley of the Rhine; but the only symbol for happiness I know is a wide prospect all golden in the setting sun, with a shining stream of silver running through it, like the path of life or like the ideal that guides you through it, and far away the grey towers of an ancient town.

XLVII

FAILURE

ALITTLE man, portly, in a fantastic hat, like a bushranger's, with an immense brim, a pea-jacket such as you see in Leech's pictures of the sea-faring man, and very wide check trousers of a cut fashionable heaven knows how many years ago. When he takes off his hat you see a fine head of long curly hair, and though he is approaching the sixties it is scarcely grey. His features are regular. He wears a collar several sizes too large for him so that his whole neck, massive and statuesque, is shown. He has the look of a Roman Emperor in a tragedy of the sixties and this air of an actor of the old school is enhanced by his deep booming voice. His stumpy frame makes it slightly absurd. You can imagine his declaiming the blank verse of Sheridan Knowles with an emphasis to rouse the pit to frenzy, and when he greets you, with too large a gesture, you guess how that resonant organ would tremble when he wrung your heart (in 1860) over the death of his child. It was splendid a little later to hear him ask the Chinese servant for "me boots, boy, me boots. A

kingdom for me boots." He confessed that he
should have been an actor.

"To be or not to be, that was the question, but
me family, me family, dear boy, they would have
died of the disgrace, and so I was exposed to the
slings and arrows of outrageous fortune."

In short he came out to China as a tea-taster.
But he came when the Ceylon tea was already
ousting the Chinese and it was no longer possible
for the merchant to enrich himself in a few years.
But the old lavishness endured and life was led in
a grand style when the means to pay for it no
longer existed. The struggle became harder.
Finally came the Sino-Japanese war, and with the
loss of Formosa, ruin. The tea-taster looked
about for other means of livelihood. He became
a wine-merchant, an undertaker, an estate-agent,
a broker, an auctioneer. He tried every way of
making money that his ardent imagination suggested, but with the diminishing prosperity of the
port his efforts were bootless. Life was too much
for him. And now at last he had the pitiful air of
a broken man; there was even something touching
in it, like the appeal of a woman who cannot believe in the loss of her beauty and implores the
compliment which reassures but no longer con-
vinces her. And yet, notwithstanding, he had a
solace: he had still a magnificent assurance; he
was a failure and he knew it; but it did not really
affect him, for he was the victim of fate: no
shadow of a doubt in his own capacity had ever
crossed his mind.

XLVIII

A STUDENT OF THE DRAMA

H E sent in a neat card of the correct shape and size, deeply bordered in black, upon which under his name was printed *Professor of Comparative Modern Literature.* He turned out to be a young man, small, with tiny elegant hands, with a larger nose than you see as a rule in the Chinese and gold rimmed spectacles. Though it was a warm day he was dressed, in European clothes, in a suit of heavy tweed. He seemed a trifle shy. He spoke in a high falsetto, as though his voice had never broken, and those shrill notes gave I know not what feeling of unreality to his conversation. He had studied in Geneva and in Paris, Berlin and Vienna, and he expressed himself fluently in English, French, and German.

It appeared that he lectured on the drama and he had lately written, in French, a work on the Chinese theatre. His studies abroad had left him with a surprising enthusiasm for Scribe, and this was the model he proposed for the regeneration of the Chinese drama. It was curious to hear him demand that the drama should be exciting. He was asking for the *pièce bien faite,* the *scène*

188

à faire, the curtain, the unexpected, the dramatic.
The Chinese theatre, with its elaborate symbolism,
has been what we are always crying for, the theatre
of ideas; and apparently it has been perishing of
dullness. It is true that ideas do not grow on
every gooseberry bush, they need novelty to make
them appetising, and when they are stale they
stink as badly as stale fish.

But then, remembering the description on the
card, I asked my friend what books, English and
French, he recommended his students to read in
order to familiarise themselves with the current
literature of the day. He hesitated a little.

"I really don't know," he said at last, "you see,
that's not my branch, I only have to do with
drama; but if you're interested I'll ask my col-
league who lectures on European fiction to call
on you."

"I beg your pardon," I said.

"Have you read *Les Avariés?*" he asked. "I
think that is the finest play that has been produced in Europe since Scribe."

"Do you?" I said politely.

"Yes, you see our students are greatly interested in sociological questions."

It is my misfortune that I am not, and so as
deftly as I could I led the conversation to Chinese
philosophy which I was desultorily reading. I
mentioned Chuang-Tzu. The professor's jaw fell.

"He lived a very long time ago," he said, per-
plexed.

"So did Aristotle," I murmured pleasantly.

189

"I have never studied the philosophers," he said, "but of course we have at our university a professor of Chinese philosophy and if you are interested in that I will ask him to come and call on you."

It is useless to argue with a pedagogue, as the Spirit of the Ocean (somewhat portentously to my mind) remarked to the Spirit of the River and I resigned myself to discuss the drama. My professor was interested in its technique and indeed was preparing a course of lectures on the subject, which he seemed to think both complicated and abstruse. He flattered me by asking me what were the secrets of the craft.

"I know only two," I answered. "One is to have common-sense and the other is to stick to the point."

"Does it require no more than that to write a play?" he inquired with a shade of dismay in his tone.

"You want a certain knack," I allowed, "but no more than to play billiards."

"They lecture on the technique of the drama in all the important universities of America," said he.

"The Americans are an extremely practical people," I answered. "I believe that Harvard is instituting a chair to instruct grandmothers how to suck eggs."

"I do not think I quite understand you."

"If you can't write a play no one can teach

190

you and if you can it's as easy as falling off a log."

Here his face expressed a lively perplexity, but I think only because he could not make up his mind whether this operation came within the province of the professor of physics or within that of the professor of applied mechanics.

"But if it is so easy to write a play why do dramatists take so long about it?"

"They didn't, you know. Lope de la Vega and Shakespeare and a hundred others wrote copiously and with ease. Some modern playwrights have been perfectly illiterate men and have found it an almost insuperable difficulty to put two sentences together. A celebrated English dramatist once showed me a manuscript and I saw that he had written the question: will you have sugar in your tea, five times before he could put it in this form. A novelist would starve if he could not on the whole say what he wanted to without any beating about the bush."

"You would not call Ibsen an illiterate man and yet it is well known that he took two years to write a play."

"It is obvious that Ibsen found a prodigious difficulty in thinking of a plot. He racked his brain furiously, month after month, and at last in despair used the very same that he had used before."

"What do you mean?" the professor cried, his voice rising to a shrill scream. "I do not understand you at all."

191

"Have you not noticed that Ibsen uses the same plot over and over again? A number of people are living in a closed and stuffy room, then some one comes (from the mountains or from over the sea) and flings the window open; everyone gets a cold in the head and the curtain falls."

I thought it just possible that the shadow of a smile might lighten for a moment the professor's grave face, but he knit his brows and gazed for two minutes into space. Then he rose.

"I will peruse the works of Henrik Ibsen once more with that point of view in mind," he said.

I did not omit before he left to put him the question which one earnest student of the drama always puts another when peradventure they meet. I asked him, namely, what he thought was the future of the theatre. I had an idea that he said, oh hell, but on reflection I believe his exclamation must have been, ô ciel! He sighed, he shook his head, he threw up his elegant hands; he looked the picture of dejection. It was certainly a comfort to find that all thoughtful people considered the drama's state in China no less desperate than all thoughtful people consider it in England.

XLIX

THE TAIPAN

NO one knew better than he that he was an important person. He was number one in not the least important branch of the most important English firm in China. He had worked his way up through solid ability and he looked back with a faint smile at the callow clerk who had come out to China thirty years before. When he remembered the modest home he had come from, a little red house in a long row of little red houses, in Barnes, a suburb which, aiming desperately at the genteel, achieves only a sordid melancholy, and compared it with the magnificent stone mansion, with its wide verandahs and spacious rooms, which was at once the office of the company and his own residence, he chuckled with satisfaction. He had come a long way since then. He thought of the high tea to which he sat down when he came home from school (he was at St. Paul's), with his father and mother and his two sisters, a slice of cold meat, a great deal of bread and butter and plenty of milk in his tea, everybody helping himself, and then he thought of the state in which now he ate his evening meal. He always dressed and whether he was alone or

not he expected the three boys to wait at table.
His number one boy knew exactly what he liked
and he never had to bother himself with the details
of housekeeping; but he always had a set dinner
with soup and fish, entree, roast, sweet and sav-
oury, so that if he wanted to ask anyone in at the
last moment he could. He liked his food and he
did not see why when he was alone he should have
less good a dinner than when he had a guest.

He had indeed gone far. That was why he did
not care to go home now, he had not been to
England for ten years, and he took his leave in
Japan or Vancouver where he was sure of meeting
old friends from the China coast. He knew no one
at home. His sisters had married in their own
station, their husbands were clerks and their sons
were clerks; there was nothing between him and
them; they bored him. He satisfied the claims of
relationship by sending them every Christmas a
piece of fine silk, some elaborate embroidery, or
a case of tea. He was not a mean man and as
long as his mother lived he had made her an allowance. But when the time came for him to retire
he had no intention of going back to England, he
had seen too many men do that and he knew how
often it was a failure; he meant to take a house
near the race-course in Shanghai: what with
bridge and his ponies and golf he expected to get
through the rest of his life very comfortably. But
he had a good many years before he need think
of retiring. In another five or six Higgins
would be going home and then he would take

charge of the head office in Shanghai. Meanwhile he was very happy where he was, he could save money, which you couldn't do in Shanghai, and have a good time into the bargain. This place had another advantage over Shanghai: he was the most prominent man in the community and what he said went. Even the consul took care to keep on the right side of him. Once a consul and he had been at loggerheads and it was not he who had gone to the wall. The taipan thrust out his jaw pugnaciously as he thought of the incident.

But he smiled, for he felt in an excellent humour. He was walking back to his office from a capital luncheon at the Hong-Kong and Shanghai Bank. They did you very well there. The food was first rate and there was plenty of liquor. He had started with a couple of cocktails, then he had some excellent sauterne and he had finished up with two glasses of port and some fine old brandy. He felt good. And when he left he did a thing that was rare with him; he walked. His bearers with his chair kept a few paces behind him in case he felt inclined to slip into it, but he enjoyed stretching his legs. He did not get enough exercise these days. Now that he was too heavy to ride it was difficult to get exercise. But if he was too heavy to ride he could still keep ponies, and as he strolled along in the balmy air he thought of the spring meeting. He had a couple of griffins that he had hopes of and one of the lads in his office had turned out a fine jockey (he must see they didn't sneak him away, old Higgins in Shanghai would give a pot of money to get him over there) and he ought to pull off two or three races. He flattered himself that he had the finest stable in the city. He pouted his broad chest like a pigeon. It was a beautiful day, and it was good to be alive.

He paused as he came to the cemetery. It stood there, neat and orderly, as an evident sign of the community's opulence. He never passed the cemetery without a little glow of pride. He was pleased to be an Englishman. For the cemetery stood in a place, valueless when it was chosen, which with the increase of the city's affluence was now worth a great deal of money. It had been suggested that the graves should be moved to another spot and the land sold for building, but the feeling of the community was against it. It gave the taipan a sense of satisfaction to think that their dead rested on the most valuable site on the island. It showed that there were things they cared for more than money. Money be blowed! When it came to "the things that mattered" (this was a favourite phrase with the taipan) well, one remembered that money wasn't everything.

And now he thought he would take a stroll through. He looked at the graves. They were neatly kept and the pathways were free from weeds. There was a look of prosperity. And as he sauntered along he read the names on the tombstones. Here were three side by side; the captain, the first mate, and the second mate of the barque *Mary Baxter*, who had all perished together in the typhoon of 1908. He remembered it well.

196

There was a little group of two missionaries, their
wives and children, who had been massacred during
the Boxer troubles. Shocking thing that had
been! Not that he took much stock in missionaries; but, hang it all, one couldn't have these
damned Chinese massacring them. Then he came
to a cross with a name on it he knew. Good chap,
Edward Mulock, but he couldn't stand his liquor,
drank himself to death, poor devil, at twenty-five:
the taipan had known a lot of them do that; there
were several more neat crosses with a man's name
on them and the age, twenty-five, twenty-six, or
twenty-seven; it was always the same story; they
had come out to China: they had never seen so
much money before, they were good fellows and
they wanted to drink with the rest: they couldn't
stand it, and there they were in the cemetery. You
had to have a strong head and a fine constitution
to drink drink for drink on the China coast. Of
course it was very sad, but the taipan could hardly
help a smile when he thought how many of those
young fellows he had drunk underground. And
there was a death that had been useful, a fellow
in his own firm, senior to him and a clever chap
too: if that fellow had lived he might not have
been taipan now. Truly the ways of fate were
inscrutable. Ah, and here was little Mrs. Turner,
Violet Turner, she had been a pretty little thing,
he had had quite an affair with her; he had been
devilish cut up when she died. He looked at her
age on the tombstone. She'd be no chicken if she
were alive now. And as he thought of all those

dead people a sense of satisfaction spread through him. He had beaten them all. They were dead and he was alive, and by George he'd scored them off. His eyes collected in one picture all those crowded graves and he smiled scornfully. He very nearly rubbed his hands.

"No one ever thought I was a fool," he muttered.

He had a feeling of good-natured contempt for the gibbering dead. Then, as he strolled along, he came suddenly upon two coolies digging a grave. He was astonished, for he had not heard that anyone in the community was dead.

"Who the devil's that for?" he said aloud.

The coolies did not even look at him, they went on with their work, standing in the grave, deep down, and they shovelled up heavy clods of earth. Though he had been so long in China he knew no Chinese, in his day it was not thought necessary to learn the damned language, and he asked the coolies in English whose grave they were digging. They did not understand. They answered him in Chinese and he cursed them for ignorant fools. He knew that Mrs. Broome's child was ailing and it might have died, but he would certainly have heard of it, and besides that wasn't a child's grave, it was a man's and a big man's too. It was uncanny. He wished he hadn't gone into that cemetery; he hurried out and stepped into his chair. His good humour had all gone and there was an uneasy frown on his face. The moment he got back to his office he called to his number two:

"I say, Peters, who's dead, d'you know?"

But Peters knew nothing. The taipan was puzzled. He called one of the native clerks and sent him to the cemetery to ask the coolies. He began to sign his letters. The clerk came back and said the coolies had gone and there was no one to ask. The taipan began to feel vaguely annoyed: he did not like things to happen of which he knew nothing. His own boy would know, his boy always knew everything, and he sent for him; but the boy had heard of no death in the community.

"I knew no one was dead," said the taipan irritably. "But what's the grave for?"

He told the boy to go to the overseer of the cemetery and find out what the devil he had dug a grave for when no one was dead.

"Let me have a whisky and soda before you go," he added, as the boy was leaving the room.

He did not know why the sight of the grave had made him uncomfortable. But he tried to put it out of his mind. He felt better when he had drunk the whisky, and he finished his work. He went upstairs and turned over the pages of *Punch*. In a few minutes he would go to the club and play a rubber or two of bridge before dinner. But it would ease his mind to hear what his boy had to say and he waited for his return. In a little while the boy came back and he brought the overseer with him.

"What are you having a grave dug for?" he asked the overseer point blank. "Nobody's dead."

"I no dig glave," said the man.

"What the devil do you mean by that? There were two coolies digging a grave this afternoon."

The two Chinese looked at one another. Then the boy said they had been to the cemetery together. There was no new grave there.

The taipan only just stopped himself from speaking.

"But damn it all, I saw it myself," were the words on the tip of his tongue.

But he did not say them. He grew very red as he choked them down. The two Chinese looked at him with their steady eyes. For a moment his breath failed him.

"All right. Get out," he gasped.

But as soon as they were gone he shouted for the boy again, and when he came, maddeningly impassive, he told him to bring some whisky. He rubbed his sweating face with a handkerchief. His hand trembled when he lifted the glass to his lips. They could say what they liked, but he had seen the grave. Why, he could hear still the dull thud as the coolies threw the spadefuls of earth on the ground above them. What did it mean? He could feel his heart beating. He felt strangely ill at ease. But he pulled himself together. It was all nonsense. If there was no grave there it must have been an hallucination. The best thing he could do was to go to the club, and if he ran across the doctor he would ask him to give him a look over.

Everyone in the club looked just the same as ever. He did not know why he should have ex-

pected them to look different. It was a comfort.
These men, living for many years with one another
lives that were methodically regulated, had acquired a number of little idiosyncrasies—one of
them hummed incessantly while he played bridge,
another insisted on drinking beer through a straw
—and these tricks which had so often irritated the
taipan now gave him a sense of security. He
needed it, for he could not get out of his head that
strange sight he had seen; he played bridge very
badly; his partner was censorious, and the taipan
lost his temper. He thought the men were looking
at him oddly. He wondered what they saw in
him that was unaccustomed.

Suddenly he felt he could not bear to stay in
the club any longer. As he went out he saw the
doctor reading *The Times* in the reading-room,
but he could not bring himself to speak to him.
He wanted to see for himself whether that grave
was really there and stepping into his chair he
told his bearers to take him to the cemetery. You
couldn't have an hallucination twice, could you?
And besides, he would take the overseer in with
him and if the grave was not there he wouldn't
see it, and if it was he'd give the overseer the
soundest thrashing he'd ever had. But the overseer was nowhere to be found. He had gone out
and taken the keys with him. When the taipan
found he could not get into the cemetery he felt
suddenly exhausted. He got back into his chair
and told his bearers to take him home. He would
lie down for half an hour before dinner. He was

tired out. That was it. He had heard that people had hallucinations when they were tired. When his boy came in to put out his clothes for dinner it was only by an effort of will that he got up. He had a strong inclination not to dress that evening, but he resisted it: he made it a rule to dress, he had dressed every evening for twenty years and it would never do to break his rule. But he ordered a bottle of champagne with his dinner and that made him feel more comfortable. Afterwards he told the boy to bring him the best brandy. When he had drunk a couple of glasses of this he felt himself again. Hallucinations be damned! He went to the billiard room and practised a few difficult shots. There could not be much the matter with him when his eye was so sure. When he went to bed he sank immediately into a sound sleep.

But suddenly he awoke. He had dreamed of that open grave and the coolies digging leisurely. He was sure he had seen them. It was absurd to say it was an hallucination when he had seen them with his own eyes. Then he heard the rattle of the night watchman going his rounds. It broke upon the stillness of the night so harshly that it made him jump out of his skin. And then terror seized him. He felt a horror of the winding multitudinous streets of the Chinese city, and there was something ghastly and terrible in the convoluted roofs of the temples with their devils grimacing and tortured. He loathed the smells that assaulted his nostrils. And the people. Those myriads of blue clad coolies, and the beggars in their filthy rags, and the merchants and the magistrates, sleek, smiling, and inscrutable, in their long black gowns. They seemed to press upon him with menace. He hated the country. China. Why had he ever come? He was panic-stricken now. He must get out. He would not stay another year, another month. What did he care about Shanghai?

"Oh, my God," he cried, "if I were only safely back in England."

He wanted to go home. If he had to die he wanted to die in England. He could not bear to be buried among all these yellow men, with their slanting eyes and their grinning faces. He wanted to be buried at home, not in that grave he had seen that day. He could never rest there. Never. What did it matter what people thought? Let them think what they liked. The only thing that mattered was to get away while he had the chance.

He got out of bed and wrote to the head of the firm and said he had discovered he was dangerously ill. He must be replaced. He could not stay longer than was absolutely necessary. He must go home at once.

They found the letter in the morning clenched in the taipan's hand. He had slipped down between the desk and the chair. He was stone dead.

L

METEMPSYCHOSIS

HE was decently though far from richly clad. He had a small round cap of black silk on his head, and on his feet black silk shoes. His robe was pale green of the flowered silk which is made in Chiating, and over it he wore a short black jacket. He was an old man, with a white beard, long and for a Chinese full; his broad face, much wrinkled, especially between the brows, was benign, and his large horn spectacles did not conceal the friendliness of his eyes. He had all the look of one of those sages whom you may see in an old picture seated by a bamboo grove at the foot of a great rocky mountain contemplating the Eternal Way. But now his face bore an expression of great annoyance and his kindly eyes were frowning, for he was engaged in the singular occupation (for a man of his appearance) of leading a little black pig along the causeway between the flooded padi fields. And the little black pig, with sudden jerks, with unexpected dodging, ran hither and thither, in every direction but that in which the old gentleman wished to go. He pulled the string violently, but the pig, squealing, refused to follow; he addressed it in terms of expostulation and of abuse, but the little pig sat on his haunches and looked at him with malicious eyes. Then I knew that in the Tang dynasty the old gentleman had been a philosopher who had juggled with facts, as philosophers will, making them suit the whims which he called his theories; and now, after who knows how many existences, he was expiating his sins in suffering in his turn the stubborn tyranny of the facts which he had outraged.

THE FRAGMENT

WHEN you travel in China I think nothing amazes you more than the passion for decoration which possesses the Chinese. It is not astonishing that you should find decoration in memorial arches or in temples; here the occasion for it is obvious; and it is natural enough to find it in furniture; nor does it surprise, though it delights you, to discover it on the commoner objects of household use. The pewter pot is enriched with a graceful design; the coolie's rice bowl has its rough but not inelegant adornment. You may fancy that the Chinese craftsman does not look upon an article as complete till by line or colour he has broken the plainness of a surface. He will even print an arabesque on the paper he uses for wrapping. But it is more unexpected when you see the elaborate embellishment of a shop-front, the splendid carving, gilt or relieved with gold, of its counter, and the intricate sculpture of the sign-board. It may be that this magnificence serves as an advertisement; but it does so only because the passer-by, the possible customer, takes pleasure in elegance; and you are apt to think that the tradesman who owns the shop takes pleasure in it too. When he sits at his door, smoking his water pipe and through his great horn spectacles reading a newspaper, his eyes must rest with good humour sometimes on the fantastic ornamentation. On the counter, in a long-necked pot, stands a solitary carnation.

You will find the same delight in the ornate in the poorest villages where the severity of a door is mitigated by a charming piece of carving, and where the trellis of the windows forms a complicated and graceful pattern. You can seldom cross a bridge, in however unfrequented a district, without seeing in it the hand of an artist. The stones are so laid as to make an intricate decoration, and it seems as though these singular people judged with a careful eye whether a flat bridge or an arched one would fit in best with the surrounding scene. The balustrade is ornamented with lions or with dragons. I remember a bridge that must have been placed just where it was for the pure delight of its beauty rather than for any useful purpose, since, though broad enough for a carriage and pair to pass over it, it served only to connect a narrow path that led from one ragged village to another. The nearest town was thirty miles away. The broad river, narrowing at this point, flowed between two green hills, and nut trees grew on the bank. The bridge had no balustrade. It was constructed of immense slabs of granite and rested on five piers; the middle pier consisted of a huge and fantastic dragon with a long and scaly tail. On the sides of the outer slabs, running the whole length of the bridge, was cut in very low relief a pattern of an unimaginable lightness, delicacy and grace.

But though the Chinese take such careful pains to avoid fatiguing your eye, with sure taste making the elaborateness of a decoration endurable by contrasting it with a plain surface, in the end weariness overcomes you. Their exuberance bewilders. You cannot refuse your admiration to the ingenuity with which they so diversify the ideas that occupy them as to give you an impression of changing fantasy, but the fact is plain that the ideas are few. The Chinese artist is like a fiddler who with infinite skill should play infinite variations upon a single tune.

Now, I happened upon a French doctor who had been in practice for many years in the city in which I then found myself; and he was a collector of porcelain, bronze, and embroidery. He took me to see his things. They were beautiful, but they were a trifle monotonous. I admired perfunctorily. Suddenly I came upon the fragment of a bust.

"But that is Greek," I said, in surprise.

"Do you think so? I am glad to hear you say it."

Head and arms were gone, and the statue, for such it had been, was broken off just above the waist, but there was a breastplate, with a sun in the middle of it, and in relief Perseus killing the dragon. It was a fragment of no great importance, but it was Greek, and perhaps because I was surfeited with Chinese beauty it affected me strangely. It spoke in a tongue with which I was familiar. It rested my heart. I passed my hands over its age-worn surface with a delight I was myself surprised at. I was like a sailor who, wandering in a tropic sea, has known the lazy loveliness of coral islands and the splendours of the cities of the East, but finds himself once more in the dingy alleys of a Channel port. It is cold and grey and sordid, but it is England.

The doctor—he was a little bald man, with gleaming eyes and an excitable manner—rubbed his hands.

"Do you know it was found within thirty miles of here, on this side of the Tibetan frontier?"

"Found!" I exclaimed. "Found where?"

"*Mon Dieu*, in the ground. It had been buried for two thousand years. They found this and several fragments more, one or two complete statues, I believe, but they were broken up and only this remained."

It was incredible that Greek statues should have been discovered in so remote a spot.

"But what is your explanation?" I asked.

"I think this was a statue of Alexander," he said.

"By George!"

It was a thrill. Was it possible that one of the commanders of the Macedonian, after the expedition into India, had found his way into this mysterious corner of China under the shadow of the

mountains of Tibet? The doctor wanted to show
me Manchu dresses, but I could not give them my
attention. What bold adventurer was he who had
penetrated so far towards the East to found a
kingdom? There he had built a temple to Aphro-
dite and a temple to Dionysus, and in the theatre
actors had sung the Antigone and in his halls at
night bards had recited the Odyssey. And he and
his men listening may have felt themselves the peers
of the old seaman and his followers. What magnificence did that stained fragment of marble call
up and what fabulous adventures! How long had
the kingdom lasted and what tragedy marked its
fall? Ah, just then I could not look at Tibetan
banners or celadon cups; for I saw the Parthenon,
severe and lovely, and beyond, serene, the blue
Ægean.

LII

ONE OF THE BEST

I COULD never remember his name, but whenever he was spoken of in the port he was always described as one of the best. He was a man of fifty perhaps, thin and rather tall, dapper and well-dressed, with a small, neat head and sharp features. His blue eyes were good-natured and jovial behind his pince-nez. He was of a cheerful disposition, and he had a vein of banter which was not ineffective. He could turn out the sort of jokes that make men standing at the club bar laugh heartily, and he could be agreeably malicious, but without ill-nature, about any member of the community who did not happen to be present. His humour was of the same nature as that of the comedian in a musical play. When they spoke of him they often said:

"You know, I wonder he never went on the stage. He'd have made a hit. One of the best."

He was always ready to have a drink with you and no sooner was your glass empty than he was prompt with the China phrase:

"Ready for the other half?"

But he did not drink more than was good for him.

"Oh, he's got his head screwed on his shoulders the right way," they said. "One of the best."

When the hat was passed round for some charitable object he could always be counted on to give as much as anyone else, and he was always ready to go in for a golf competition or a billiards tournament. He was a bachelor.

"Marriage is no use to a man who lives in China," he said. "He has to send his wife away every summer and then when the kids are beginning to be interesting they have to go home. It costs a deuce of a lot of money and you get nothing out of it."

But he was always willing to do a good turn to any woman in the community. He was number one at Jardine's, and he often had the power to make himself useful. He had been in China for thirty years, and he prided himself on not speaking a word of Chinese. He never went into the Chinese city. His compradore was Chinese, and some of the clerks, his boys of course, and the chair coolies; but they were the only Chinese he had anything to do with, and quite enough too.

"I hate the country, I hate the people," he said. "As soon as I've saved enough money I mean to clear out."

He laughed.

"Do you know, last time I was home I found everyone cracked over Chinese junk, pictures and porcelain, and stuff. Don't talk to me about Chinese things, I said to 'em. I never want to see anything Chinese as long as I live."

212

He turned to me.

"I'll tell you what, I don't believe I've got a single Chinese thing in my house."

But if you wanted him to talk to you about London he was prepared to do so by the hour. He knew all the musical comedies that had been played for twenty years and at the distance of nine thousand miles he was able to keep up with the doings of Miss Lily Elsie and Miss Elsie Janis. He played the piano and he had a pleasing voice; it required little persuasion to induce him to sit down and sing you the popular ditties he had heard when last he was at home. It was quite singular to me, the unfathomable frivolity of this grey-haired man; it was even a little uncanny. But people applauded him loudly when he finished.

"He's priceless, isn't he?" they said. "Oh, one of the best."

LIII

THE SEA-DOG

SHIPS' captains for the most part are very dull men. Their conversation is of freights and cargoes. They have seen little more in the ports they visit than their agent's office, the bar which their kind frequents, and the bawdy houses. They owe the glamour of romance which their connection with the sea has cast over them to the imagination of the landsman. To them the sea is a means of livelihood and they know it, as an engine-driver knows his engine, from a standpoint which is aridly practical. They are men, working men, of a narrow outlook, with small education for the most part and little culture; they are all of a piece, and they have neither subtlety nor imagination. Straightforward, courageous, honest, and reliable, they stand four-square on the immutability of the obvious; and they are definite: they are placed in their surroundings like the objects in a stereoscopic photograph so that you seem to see all round them. They offer themselves to you with salient traits.

But no one could have adhered less to type than Captain Boots. He was the master of a little.

Chinese steamer on the Upper Yangtze and because I was his only passenger we spent a good deal of time in one another's company. But though he was fluent of speech, garrulous even, I see him shadowly; and he remains in my mind indistinctly. I suppose it is on account of his elusiveness that he engages my imagination. There was certainly nothing elusive in his appearance. He was a big man, six foot two, powerfully built, with large features and a red, friendly face. When he laughed he showed a row of handsome gold teeth. He was very bald, and clean-shaven; but he had the most bushy, abundant, and aggressive eyebrows that I have ever seen, and under them mild blue eyes. He was a Dutchman and though he had left Holland when he was eight, he still spoke with an accent. He could not pronounce th, but always made it d. His father, a fisherman who sailed his own schooner on the Zuyder Zee, hearing that fishing was good in Newfoundland, had set out with his wife and his two sons across the broad Atlantic. After some years there and in Hudson's Bay—all this was hard on half a century ago—they had sailed round the Horn for the Behring Straits. They hunted seal until the law stepped in to save the beasts they were exterminating, and then Boots, a man now and a brave one, God knows, sailed here and there, as third, then as second mate, on sailing vessels. He had been almost all his life in sail and now on a steamer could not make himself at home.

"It's only in a sailing boat you get comfort," he said. "Dere's no comfort anywhere when you got steam."

He had been all along the coast of South America after nitrates, then to the west coast of Africa, then again, fishing cod off the coast of Maine, to America; and after that with cargoes of salt fish to Spain and Portugal. A tavern acquaintance in Manila suggested that he should try the Chinese Customs. He went to Hong-Kong, where he was taken on as a tide-waiter, and presently was put in command of a steam launch. He spent three years, chasing the opium smugglers, and then, having saved a little money, built himself a forty-five ton schooner with which he determined to go to the Behring Straits and try his luck again with the seal fishery.

"But I guess my crew got scared," he said. "When I got to Shanghai they deserted and I couldn't get no oder, so I had to sell de boat and I shipped on a vessel what was going to Vancouver."

It was then he first left the sea. He met a man who was pushing a patent hay-fork and this he agreed to take round the States. It was a queer occupation for a sailor-man, and it was not a successful one, for at Salt Lake City, the firm that employed him having gone bankrupt, he found himself stranded. Somehow or other he got back to Vancouver, but he was taken with the idea of life ashore, and he found work with an estate-agent. It was his duty to take the purchasers of land to their plots and if they were not satisfied persuade them that they need not regret their bargain.

"We sold one fellow a farm on de side of a mountain," he said, his blue eyes twinkling at the recollection, "an' it was so steep dat de chickens had one leg longer dan de oder."

After five years he had the idea that he would like to go back to China. He had no difficulty in getting a job as mate of a ship sailing west and soon he was at the old life once more. Since then he had been on most of the China runs, from Vladivostok to Shanghai, from Amoy to Manila, and on all the big rivers; on steamers now, rising from second to first mate, and at last, on Chinese owned ships, to master. He talked willingly of his plans for the future. He had been in China long enough, and he hankered after a farm on the Fraser River. He would build himself a boat and do a bit of fishing, salmon and halibut.

"It's time I settled down," he said. "Fifty-dree years I've been to sea. An' I shouldn't wonder but what I did a bit of boat building too. I'm not one to stick to one ding."

There he was right and this restlessness of his translated itself into a curious indecision of character. There was something fluid about him so that you did not know where to take hold of him. He reminded you of a scene of mist and rain in a Japanese print where the design, barely suggested, almost escapes you. He had a peculiar gentleness which was somewhat unexpected in the rough old salt.

"I don't want to offend anyone," he said. "Treat 'em kindly, dat's what I try to do. If people won't do what you want talk to 'em nicely, persuade 'em. Dere's no need to be nasty. Try what coaxing'll do."

It was a principle which it was unusual to find used with the Chinese, and I do not know that it answered very well, for after some difficulty he would come into the cabin, wave his hands, and say:

"I can do noding wid dem. Dey won't listen to reason."

And then his moderation looked very like weakness. But he was no fool. He had a sense of humour. At one place we were drawing over seven feet and since the river at its shallowest was barely that and the course was dangerous the harbour authorities would not give us our papers till part of the cargo was unloaded. It was the ship's last trip and she was carrying the pay of regiments stationed several days down stream. The military governor refused to let the ship start unless the bullion was taken.

"I guess I got to do what you tell me," said Captain Boots to the harbour master.

"You don't get your papers till I see the five foot mark above the water," answered the harbour master.

"I'll tell the compradore to take out some of dat silver."

He took the harbour master up to the Customs'
Club and stood him drinks while this was being
done. He drank with him for four hours, and
when he returned he walked as steadily as when
he went. But the harbour-master was drunk.

"Ah, I see dey've got it down two foot," said
Captain Boots. "Dat's all right den."

The harbour-master looked at the numbers on
the ship's side and sure enough the five foot mark
was at the water's edge.

"That's good," he said. "And now you can
go."

"I'll be off right away," said the captain.

Not a pound of cargo had been removed, but an
astute Chinaman had neatly repainted the numbers.

And later when mutinous regiments with an eye
on the silver we carried sought to prevent us from
leaving one of the riverside cities he showed an
agreeable firmness. His equable temper was tried
and he said:

"No one's going to make me stay where I don't
want to. I'm de master of dis ship and I'm de
man what gives de orders. I'm going."

The agitated compradore said the military
would fire if we attempted to move. An officer
uttered a command and the soldiers, going down
on one knee, levelled their rifles. Captain Boots
looked at them.

"Put down de bullet proof screen," he said. "I
tell you I'm going and de Chinese army can go to
hell."

He gave his orders to raise the anchor and at the same time the officer gave the order to fire. Captain Boots stood on his bridge, a somewhat grotesque figure, for in his old blue jersey, with his red face and burly frame, he looked the very image of those ancient fishermen that you see lounging about Grimsby docks, and he rang his bell. We steamed out slowly to the spatter of rifle shots.

LIV

THE QUESTION

THEY took me to the temple. It stood on the side of a hill with a semi-circle of tawny mountains behind it, staging it, as it were, with a formal grandeur; and they pointed out to me with what exquisite art the series of buildings climbed the hill till you reached the final edifice, a jewel of white marble encircled by the trees; for the Chinese architect sought to make his creation an ornament to nature and he used the accidents of the landscape to complete his decorative scheme. They pointed out to me how cunningly the trees were planted to contrast with the marble of a gateway, to give an agreeable shadow here, or there to serve as a background; and they made me remark the admirable proportion of those great roofs, rising one beyond the other, in rich profusion, with the grace of flowers; and they showed me that the yellow tiles were of different hues so that the sensibility was not offended by an expanse of colour but amused and pleased by a subtle variety of tone. They showed me how the elaborate carving of a gateway was contrasted with a surface without adornment so that the eye was not wearied. All this they showed me as we walked through elegant courtyards, over bridges which were a miracle of grace, through temples with strange gods, dark and gesticulating; but when I asked them what was the spiritual state which had caused all this mass of building to be made, they could not tell me.

LV

THE SINOLOGUE

H E is a tall man, rather stout, flabby as
though he does not take enough exercise, with a red, clean-shaven, broad
face and grey hair. He talks very
quickly, in a nervous manner, with a voice not
quite big enough for his body. He lives in a
temple just outside the city gate, inhabiting the
guest chambers, and three Buddhist priests, with
a tiny acolyte, tend the temple and conduct the
rites. There is a little Chinese furniture in the
rooms and a vast number of books, but no comfort.
It is cold and the study in which we sit is insuf-
ficiently warmed by a petroleum stove.

He knows more Chinese than any man in China.
He has been working for ten years on a dictionary
which will supersede that of a noted scholar whom
for a quarter of a century he has personally dis-
liked. He is thus benefiting sinological studies and
satisfying a private grudge. He has all the manner of a don and you feel that eventually he will
be professor of Chinese at the University of Oxford and then at last exactly in his place. He is
a man of wider culture than most sinologues, who
may know Chinese, and this you must take on

trust, but who, it is lamentably obvious, know nothing else; and his conversation upon Chinese thought and literature has in consequence a fullness and a variety which you do not often find among students of the language. Because he has immersed himself in his particular pursuits and has cared nothing for racing and shooting the Europeans think him queer. They look upon him with the suspicion and awe with which human beings always regard those who do not share their tastes. They suggest that he is not quite sane and some accuse him of smoking opium. It is the charge which is always brought against the white man who has sought to familiarise himself with the civilisation in which he is to pass the greater part of his career. You have only to spend a little while in that apartment bare of the most common luxury to know that this is a man who leads a life wholly of the spirit.

But it is a specialised life. Art and beauty seem not to touch him, and as I listen to him talk so sympathetically of the Chinese poets I cannot help asking myself if the best things have not after all slipped through his fingers. Here is a man who has touched reality only through the printed page. The tragic splendour of the lotus moves him only when its loveliness is enshrined in the verse of Li Po and the laughter of demure Chinese girls stirs his blood but in the perfection of an exquisitely chiselled quatrain.

LVI

THE VICE-CONSUL

HIS bearers set down his chair in the yamen and unfastened the apron which protected him from the pouring rain. He put out his head, like a bird looking out of its nest, and then his long thin body and finally his thin long legs. He stood for a moment as if he did not quite know what to do with himself. He was a very young man and his long limbs with their ungainliness somehow added to the callowness of his air. His round face (his head looked too small for the length of his body) with its fresh complexion was quite boyish, and his pleasant brown eyes were ingenuous and candid. The sense of importance which his official position gave him (it was not long since he had been no more than a student-interpreter) struggled with his native shyness. He gave his card to the judge's secretary and was led by him into an inner court and asked to sit down. It was cold and draughty and the vice-consul was glad of his heavy waterproof. A ragged attendant brought tea and cigarettes. The secretary, an emaciated youth in a very shabby black gown, had been a student at Harvard and was glad to show off his fluent English.

Then the judge came in, and the vice-consul stood up. The judge was a portly gentleman in heavily wadded clothes, with a large smiling face and gold-rimmed spectacles. They sat down and sipped their tea and smoked American cigarettes. They chatted affably. The judge spoke no English, but the vice-consul's Chinese was fresh in his mind and he could not help thinking that he acquitted himself creditably. Presently an attendant appeared and said a few words to the judge, and the judge very courteously asked the vice-consul if he was ready for the business which had brought him. The door into the outer court was thrown open and the judge, walking through, took his place on a large seat at a table that stood at the top of the steps. He did not smile now. He had assumed instinctively the gravity proper to his office and in his walk, notwithstanding his obesity, there was an impressive dignity. The vice-consul, obeying a polite gesture, took a seat by his side. The secretary stood at the end of the table. Then the outer gateway was flung wide (it seemed to the vice-consul that there was nothing so dramatic as the opening of a door) and quickly, with an odd sort of flurry, the criminal walked in. He walked to the centre of the courtyard and stood still, facing his judge. On each side of him walked a soldier in khaki. He was a young man and the vice-consul thought that he could be no older than

226

himself. He wore only a pair of cotton trousers and a cotton singlet. They were faded but clean. He was bare-headed and bare-foot. He looked no different from any of the thousands of coolies in their monotonous blue that you passed every day in the crowded streets of the city. The judge and the criminal faced one another in silence. The vice-consul looked at the criminal's face, but then he looked down quickly: he did not want to see what was there to be seen so plainly. He felt suddenly embarrassed. And looking down he noticed how small the man's feet were, shapely and slender; his hands were tied behind his back. He was slightly built, of the middle height, a lissome creature that suggested the wild animal, and standing on those beautiful feet of his there was in his carriage a peculiar grace. But the vice-consul's eyes were drawn back unwillingly to the oval, smooth, and unlined face. It was livid. The vice-consul had often read of faces that were green with terror and he had thought it but a fanciful expression, and here he saw it. It startled him. It made him feel ashamed. And in the eyes too, eyes that did not slant as the Chinese eye is wrongly supposed always to do, but were straight, in the eyes that seemed unnaturally large and bright, fixed on those of the judge, was a terror that was horrible to see. But when the judge put him a question—trial and sentence were over and he had been brought there that morning only for purposes of identification—he answered in a loud plain voice, boldly. However his body might betray him he was still master of his will. The judge gave a brief order, and, flanked by his two soldiers, the man marched out. The judge and the vice-consul rose and walked to the gateway, where their chairs awaited them. Here stood the criminal with his guard. Notwithstanding his tied hands he smoked a cigarette. A squad of little soldiers had been sheltering themselves under the overhanging roof, and on the appearance of the judge the officer in charge made them form up. The judge and the vice-consul settled themselves in their chairs. The officer gave an order and the squad stepped out. A couple of yards behind them walked the criminal. Then came the judge in his chair and finally the vice-consul.

They went quickly through the busy streets and the shopkeepers gave the procession an incurious stare. The wind was cold and the rain fell steadily. The criminal in his cotton singlet must have been wet through. He walked with a firm step, his head held high, jauntily almost. It was some distance from the judge's yamen to the city wall and to cover it took them nearly half an hour. Then they came to the city gate and went through it. Four men in ragged blue—they looked like peasants—were standing against the wall by the side of a poor coffin, rough hewn and unpainted. The criminal gave it a glance as he passed by. The judge and the vice-consul dismounted from their chairs and the officer halted his soldiers. The rice fields began at the city wall. The criminal was led to a pathway between two patches and told to kneel down. But the officer did not think the spot suitable. He told the man to rise. He walked a yard or two and knelt down again. A soldier was detached from the squad and took up his position behind the prisoner, three feet from him perhaps; he raised his gun; the officer gave the word of command; he fired. The criminal fell forward and he moved a little, convulsively. The officer went up to him, and seeing that he was not quite dead emptied two barrels of his revolver into the body. Then he formed up his soldiers once more. The judge gave the vice-consul a smile, but it was a grimace rather than a smile; it distorted painfully that fat good-humoured face.

They stepped into their chairs; but at the city gate their ways parted; the judge bowed the vice-consul a courteous farewell. The vice-consul was carried back towards the consulate through the streets, crowded and tortuous, where life was going on just as usual. And as he went along quickly, for the consular bearers were fine fellows, his mind distracted a little by their constant shouts to make way, he thought how terrible it was to make an end of life deliberately: it seemed an immense responsibility to destroy what was the result of innumerable generations. The human race has existed so long and each one of us is here as the result of an infinite series of miraculous events. But at the same time, puzzling him, he had a sense of the triviality of life. One more or less mattered so little. But just as he reached the consulate he looked at his watch, he had no idea it was so late, and he told the bearers to take him to the club. It was time for a cocktail and by heaven he could do with one. A dozen men were standing at the bar when he went in. They knew on what errand he had been that morning.

"Well," they said, "did you see the blighter shot?"

"You bet I did," he said, in a loud and casual voice.

"Everything go off all right?"

"He wriggled a bit." He turned to the bartender. "Same as usual, John."

LVII

A CITY BUILT ON A ROCK

T HEY say of it that the dogs bark when peradventure the sun shines there. It is a grey and gloomy city, shrouded in mist, for it stands upon its rock where two great rivers meet so that it is washed on all sides but one by turbid, rushing waters. The rock is like the prow of an ancient galley and seems, as though possessed of a strange unnatural life, all tremulous with effort; it is as if it were ever on the point of forging into the tumultuous stream. Rugged mountains hem the city round about.

Outside the walls bedraggled houses are built on piles, and here, when the river is low, a hazardous population lives on the needs of the watermen; for at the foot of the rock a thousand junks are moored, wedged in with one another tightly, and men's lives there have all the turbulence of the river. A steep and tortuous stairway leads to the great gate guarded by a temple, and up and down this all day long go the water coolies, with their dripping buckets; and from their splashing the stair and the street that leads from the gate are wet as though after heavy rain. It is difficult to walk on the level for more than a few minutes, and there are as many steps as in the hill towns of the Italian Riviera. Because there is so little space the streets are pressed together, narrow and dark, and they wind continuously so that to find your way is like finding it in a labyrinth. The throng is as thick as the throng on a pavement in London when a theatre is emptying itself of its audience. You have to push your way through it, stepping aside every moment as chairs come by and coolies bearing their everlasting loads: itinerant sellers, selling almost anything that anyone can want to buy, jostle you as you pass.

The shops are wide open to the street, without windows or doors, and they are crowded too. They are like an exhibition of arts and crafts, and you may see what a street looked like in medieval England when each town made all that was necessary to its needs. The various industries are huddled together so that you will pass through a street of butchers where carcasses and entrails hang bloody on each side of you, with flies buzzing about them and mangy dogs prowling hungrily below; you will pass through a street where in each house there is a hand-loom and they are busily weaving cloth or silk. There are innumerable eating houses from which come heavy odours and here at all hours people are eating. Then, generally at a corner, you will see tea-houses, and here all day long again the tables are packed with men of all sorts drinking tea and smoking. The barbers ply their trade in the public view and you will see men leaning patiently on their crossed arms while their heads are being shaved; others are having their ears cleaned, and some, a revolting spectacle, the inside of their eyelids scraped.

It is a city of a thousand noises. There are the peddlers who announce their presence by a wooden gong; the clappers of the blind musician or of the masseuse; the shrill falsetto of a man singing in a tavern; the loud beating of a gong from a house where a wedding or a funeral is being celebrated. There are the raucous shouts of the coolies and chair-bearers; the menacing whines of the beggars, caricatures of humanity, their emaciated limbs barely covered by filthy tatters and revolting with disease; the cracked melancholy of the bugler who incessantly practises a call he can never get; and then, like a bass to which all these are a barbaric melody, the insistent sound of conversation, of people laughing, quarrelling, joking, shouting, arguing, gossiping. It is a ceaseless din. It is extraordinary at first, then confusing, exasperating, and at last maddening. You long for a moment's utter silence. It seems to you that it would be a voluptuous delight.

And then combining with the irksome throng and the din that exhausts your ears is a stench which time and experience enable you to distinguish into a thousand separate stenches. Your nostrils grow cunning. Foul odours beat upon your harassed nerves like the sound of uncouth instruments playing a horrible symphony.

You cannot tell what are the lives of these thousands who surge about you. Upon your own people sympathy and knowledge give you a hold; you can enter into their lives, at least imaginatively, and in a way really possess them. By the effort of your fancy you can make them after a fashion part of yourself. But these are as strange to you as you are strange to them. You have no clue to their mystery. For their likeness to yourself in so much does not help you; it serves rather to emphasize their difference. Someone attracts your attention, a pale youth with great horn spectacles and a book under his arm, whose studious look is pleasant, or an old man, wearing a hood, with a grey sparse beard and tired eyes: he looks like one of those sages that the Chinese artists painted in a rocky landscape or under Kang-hsi modelled in porcelain; but you might as well look at a brick wall. You have nothing to go upon, you do not know the first thing about them, and your imagination is baffled.

But when, reaching the top of the hill, you come once more to the crenellated walls that surround the city and go out through the frowning gate, you come to the graves. They stretch over the country, one mile, two miles, three, four, five, interminable green mounds, up and down the hills, with grey stones to which the people once a year come to offer libation and to tell the dead how fare the living whom they left behind; and they are as thickly crowded, the dead, as are the living in the city; and they seem to press upon the living as though they would force them into the turbid, swirling river. There is something menacing

234

about those serried ranks. It is as though they were laying siege to the city, with a sullen ruthlessness, biding their time; and as though in the end, encroaching irresistibly as fate, they would drive those seething throngs before them till the houses and the streets were covered by them, and the green mounds came down to the water gate. Then at last silence, silence would dwell there undisturbed.

They are uncanny, those green graves, they are terrifying. They seem to wait.

LVIII

A LIBATION TO THE GODS

SHE was an old woman, and her face was wizened and deeply lined. In her grey hair three long silver knives formed a fantastic headgear. Her dress of faded blue consisted of a long jacket, worn and patched, and a pair of trousers that reached a little below her calves. Her feet were bare, but on one ankle she wore a silver bangle. It was plain that she was very poor. She was not stout, but squarely built, and in her prime she must have done without effort the heavy work in which her life had been spent. She walked leisurely, with the sedate tread of an elderly woman, and she carried on her arm a basket. She came down to the harbour; it was crowded with painted junks; her eyes rested for a moment curiously on a man who stood on a narrow bamboo raft, fishing with cormorants; and then she set about her business. She put down her basket on the stones of the quay, at the water's edge, and took from it a red candle. This she lit and fixed in a chink of the stones. Then she took several joss-sticks, held each of them for a moment in the flame of the candle and set them up around it. She took three tiny bowls and filled them with a liquid that she had brought with her in a bottle and placed them neatly in a row. Then from her basket she took rolls of paper cash and paper "shoes," and unravelled them, so that they should burn easily. She made a little bonfire, and when it was well alight she took the three bowls and poured out some of their contents before the smouldering joss-sticks. She bowed herself three times and muttered certain words. She stirred the burning paper so that the flames burned brightly. Then she emptied the bowls on the stones and again bowed three times. No one took the smallest notice of her. She took a few more paper cash from her basket and flung them in the fire. Then without further ado, she took up her basket, and with the same leisurely, rather heavy tread, walked away. The gods were duly propitiated, and like an old peasant woman in France who has satisfactorily done her day's housekeeping, she went about her business.

THE END.